The Southern Awakening

A BLACK MAN'S GUIDE TO LIBERATING THE RURAL SOUTH

BARNARD SIMS

"BARNARD THE BARBER"

ARCHWAY
PUBLISHING

Archway Publishing books may be ordered through booksellers or by contacting:

Archway Publishing
1663 Liberty Drive
Bloomington, IN 47403
www.archwaypublishing.com
844-669-3957

Because of the dynamic nature of the Internet, any web addresses or links contained in this book may have changed since publication and may no longer be valid. The views expressed in this work are solely those of the author and do not necessarily reflect the views of the publisher, and the publisher hereby disclaims any responsibility for them.

Logo designed by: Miss Lacy Studios, LLC

Interior Image Credit: Dwayne Boyd Photography

Scripture taken from the King James Version of the Bible.

ISBN: 978-1-6657-1717-5 (sc)
ISBN: 978-1-6657-1718-2 (hc)
ISBN: 978-1-6657-1719-9 (e)

Library of Congress Control Number: 2021925860

Print information available on the last page.

Archway Publishing rev. date: 01/28/2022

This book is dedicated to all those who work in the service industries. Barbers, hairstylists, makeup artists, and nail technicians serve their communities as alchemists, uplifting spirits with selflessness and magically making raw pieces of iron look and feel like pure gold! I know all too well how you stand with patience. You are courteous to others while waiting for the train to clear the tracks. The time has come for you to break out and see the town's bright lights! I see your untitled masterpieces flowing through towns and cities without getting the proper recognition they each deserve. Let this book be a reminder to you that your artwork is as valuable as a painting by Jean-Michel Basquiat etched on a subway train in New York. As you selflessly serve others, remember that learning to love yourself is the greatest love of all.

This book is also dedicated to the activists who put their lives on the line for the oppressed people they love—the devoted workers in the NAACP, the National Action Network, the Black Panther Party, and other organizations who most of us have never heard of. When the world gets too bright for those who are supposed to have your back, let this book be your guiding light—proof that as long as you keep marching for righteousness, you will never walk alone.

There is no way I could be who I am today without the experiences I shared with my two brothers, two sisters-in-law (Elaine and Deborah), a darling sister, and a brother-in-law (Kenny).

To my sister, whom I affectionately call baby girl. The sun rises and sets on you. I truly adore the way you've committed your life to caring for others as a loving nurse.

And oh God, I cannot forget to tell you about my nieces and nephews! I love you all, and you make me the proudest uncle in the universe. As you look to the stars realize that you are stars too. Thus, while you are gazing on your essence, let this book prompt you to never give up on your dreams. Uncle Nard is going to buy all of you some doughnuts after my book becomes a *New York Times* best seller.

To my late father, Barney Roscoe Sims. I watched you work hard to provide for our family, and you did so even after your untimely death. You rose from the red clay of Georgia and founded the Roscoe Sims Cement Construction Company in the late 1960s.

Every important thing I would need to embrace, as a man, was set in stone by the standards you represented for me when I was just a child. It is truly the honor of my life to have been able to follow in your footsteps for the fourteen years I shared on earth with you. I am nowhere close to the man you were, but God knows I try, because I know that giving my best is what you taught me. The last thing you said to me was "Get up!" My prayer is that this book serves as a testament that I still hear your voice every day and that just as you rose from that red clay, still I rise!

To my mother, Ida B. Sims. In a world where doors are constantly slamming in the faces of black boys, the grace and mercy you've shown me has assured me the space to know I belong. Even at my worst, you have always given me your best. Your presence exemplifies God's love for me.

To my wife. I still don't know what you see in me that makes you believe I'm so smart. However, when I see you and think about how much my life has been blessed by our union, I start to believe you might be right; I am a wise man to have married you, especially since my oldest brother told me, "Don't do it. Reconsider!"

I heard my brother's advice, yet my heart for you has a life of its own. After choosing God, choosing to marry you was the best decision I've ever made. God bless your parents, my late brother-in-law Reggie (Greta), and my dear sister-in-law Angela. Without you, it wouldn't be possible for us to have the family we have.

To my mother-in-law. You are beautiful. I realize I have a lot to look forward to, being that my wife is your daughter. My father-in-law is a lucky man!

To Dan-Dan, a Bronze Star and Purple Heart Vietnam veteran. I thank you for your service and for allowing me to marry your daughter. I really appreciate that you didn't have any flashbacks or throw grenades at me when I asked for your daughter's hand. I was a little concerned about that at first, but you've embraced me as a son. We will try to guide your grandchildren to be their very best.

As we also pass down a legacy of leaving things better than they were left for us. That is what our parents, my paternal (late) grandpa and grandma—C.L. and Lona Mae—and my maternal big daddy and big ma—John Calvin and Lona Lee—did to spare us from all that they had to experience growing up in the rural South.

To our children and godchildren. I love you all without a single reservation. You are the ration that sustains me. Throughout the COVID-19 crisis, the pandemic brought us closer together as a family. And I am so thankful for the limited number of cars driving on the roads, because it allowed us to spend countless days and nights with two of our teenagers learning how to drive.

My prayer is that you will read this and be reminded of how important you are to me. It will probably be difficult for you to see past my identity as your father, your uncle, or the barber. However, you must understand that we must water you with truth because truth lights the path for the righteous way to grow. I pray this book inspires you to believe in your abilities and to know that with God, you can do all things. Believe that, and watch God grow great seeds through you.

Just a year ago, I would've never guessed I'd be writing a book, much less two of them. Use my vulnerability as your personal fuel. I am painting these pages with my soul as a reminder that if you wish to float like a butterfly, you must first be willing to break the confinements of your own cocoon. As you rise, always be the authentic version of yourself. Be your best you. You are our hopes, dreams, and aspirations. You are our resurrection!

Contents

Introduction

Many movements that have transformed America have started in musty, moldy basements of some old traditional Baptist church down south. The Mississippi movement had Fannie Lou Hamer. Alabama had John Lewis plotting movements from church pews. Cities and towns from the Carolinas to Atlanta, from Macon to Montgomery, and from Savannah through Mississippi are all deeply rooted in the archives of historical change that really made America great again.

It was Van Jones who reported that the mob of angry white people who stormed the US Capitol Building on January 6, 2021, were inspired by misinformation and mad at the idea that America might become fair and equal for people of color.

While living in the shadows of the first black president, some folks had simply had enough. It was Donald Trump, who received the fewer votes in two elections, that gaslit America's anxieties with lies. These lies were easy to disprove, yet the mad mob didn't care. After witnessing this terrorizing national embarrassment fueled by hate and intolerance for the lives of "other" people, we have to seek the water of truth to overcome this fire. Truth is the love that overcomes hate.

In the wake of this insurrection, we must galvanize a resurrection of our nation's civility. Our resurrection will require a great awakening in the people. To be specific, a southern awakening is necessary, because the South has historically been where the flames of hatred finds hosts of those safe havens.

It is this transformation that must first begin within each of us. After searching your own soul, you will find your authentic voice. Understand and believe that your unique voice has the power to activate the spirit of at least one person, somewhere in this world. With that energy, you will be primed and ready to mobilize your local community.

Through our preestablished networks, we can resurrect the South in the empowered way God has always intended. Our barbershops, beauty salons, and churches can use social networking as vehicles to revitalize even the most rural regions in the Deep South. You are not alone on Activist Island. The universe is waiting for you to cast out your voice like a smooth stone into this atmospheric equation. Be ye not afraid.

To write *The Southern Awakening*, I drew from my experiences as a civil rights activist who grew up in the South after the first couple of years of desegregation in the early 1970s. It wasn't until I was conducting research for this book, that I discovered, that I too was born in the colored side of the hospital in 1971. Now that hospital was as useless as a pile of corn shucks! Therefore, it is key that my personal awakening springs from its deep roots in the South.

The sole purpose of The Southern Awakening is to inspire dormant spaces to rise. This book is written in what I call postulates rather than chapters, for a couple of reasons. The noun *postulate* is something suggested or assumed as true as the basis for reasoning or a belief. The verb phrase *to postulate* means to suggest or assume the existence, fact, or truth of something as a basis for reasoning, discussion, or belief.

While in geometry, a postulate is a statement that is assumed true before it can be proven. Although in the spiritual realm, a postulate involves speaking goals and aspirations into existence. Yet in simple southern terms, a postulate is an educated guess. But we have to be careful about making even educated assumptions, because of the risk of looking like educated fools. (I will get more into the subject of educated fools in a later postulate.)

Anyway, when I took geometry, I developed the ability to first visualize the results as a postulate and then process the theorems in reverse as proofs. Sometimes we minimize our gifts and exaggerate our flaws. Like most, I minimized my talents.

Mostly, I attributed my abilities to my years of working as a kid with my father in his construction company. You see every day, our work involved squaring houses, figuring out square footage, and making structures parallel and perpendicular with the roads.

Therefore, by the time I started studying geometry, I was able to form postulates in my mind about the solution to a problem and then, later on, outline the proof showing that my answer was correct. Processing postulates in my mind and then working backwards worked for me.

In high school, I could show up to geometry class half asleep and still maintain a 98 average in my favorite teacher's class. Mrs. Borders' teaching methods were flexible because she understood that all students are not supposed to learn things the exact same way. I am a visual learner; seeing the process done in my head before I actually wrote down the steps was my method that worked for me.

Mrs. Borders never confined my process for formulating postulates; nor did she mind my methods for proving a theorem as long as I could show that my answer was correct, in the end. Also, my beautiful teacher was wise enough to tell me not to spend too much time trying to get others to understand my methods until I could completely articulate the reasoning behind those results.

Her logic was simply because, have you ever been asked to explain what you were doing, before you completely understood what you were doing yourself? Trying to explain what you are doing before you've had the chance to masterfully understand your process confuses everyone.

Can you imagine the first man in the barbershop trying to explain how we were going to land on the moon before we really knew it was possible? Therefore, this book is a set of eight postulates I call *A Black Man's Guide to Liberating the Rural South*. Because I believe, if we can land on the moon, surely, we can find promise in the land of the South.

Another reason I refer to postulates rather than chapters or principles is in homage to Charlamagne Tha God's *New York Times* best seller, *Black Privilege: Opportunity Comes to Those Who Create It*. The blueprint for that mind-shifting book is outlined in eight principles. While, my book to be on the best-seller list is outlined in eight postulates.

Do you see the difference? His book says McDonald's, while mine says McDowell's; they are not the same. He is Charlamagne Tha God, while I am Barnard the Barber. I repeat for copyright infringement purposes; our books are not the same!

Nonetheless, we both wrote our books with the same intent: to inspire you to create opportunities in your community. Charlamagne's book of eight principles guided me to write this book in eight postulates of my own. I hope these postulates encourage you to utilize this liberating therapy, of writing your way out of any negative circumstances you may face.

Deep within your soul, only you know your life's blueprint. An awakening involves discovering your unique voice—a system of methods, principles, or postulates, if you will. Your blueprint is designed to define the divine way that works for you.

Jimi Hendrix was one of the greatest guitar players of all times. He was left-handed but learned to play right-handed guitars upside down. Not many guitarists would dare to question Jimi Hendrix's abilities or his genius in finding a solution that worked for him. No one, not even Prince.

Therefore, it is paramount that we seek with passion to find our God-given gifts so we may light the world, in our own unique way.

While considering that, it is with upmost reverence, respect, and admiration that I mention the martyr Dr. Martin Luther King Jr. In stating that first, I must also admit that I am too nosy to be as unselfish as Dr. King was in saying, "I might not get there with you." I'm admitting right now that I am too self-centered to be cool with just getting you to the promised land if I can't go with you.

Be that as it may, most of you reading this are me-oriented humans, just as I am. Although some of you may be more reluctant than others to admit it.

We do respect the brave soldiers because of their willingness to sacrifice it all. For those qualities of honor and valor are rare, and almost unique. It takes a supreme human being to get to the mountaintop and remain content with just looking at the promised land.

Well, I don't want to just see it; I want to be in it! I want to be in the middle of that city, bathing in all its promising perks. I'm not at all certain of which Negro spiritual I'll be singing as we travel there. It will probably be one the older deacons at my church sing, such as "Come and Go to That Land." Or maybe I could sing the Mother Board's rendition of "I'm Going over Yonder."

If the choir continues singing, as they normally do in black churches, when we do get to the promised land's First Baptist Church, I'm requesting right now that we start every Easter Sunday singing, "Lord, whatever you are doing in this season, please don't do it without me. Don't do it without me!"

I not only want to make it to that land; I want to ride in the front seat!

If our communities are mobilized, we can all make it to the promised land. Mobilized political power and personal responsibility are key components to our communities' solutions.

Solutions seem complex and are often multifaceted, and sometimes they require all of the above strategies. Initially, though, communities from towns deep in the rural South must first believe in our value and our unique capabilities in order for us to make the changes we need.

The tools are at our disposal; we just have to utilize our hands to do more than just pray. Our ancestors had to hope for film crews to cover black people being mistreated or sprayed with water hoses, but we have the power to create a global viral moment by going live from our devices placed in the palms of our hands. Our elders' wisdom has been graced down, as a blessing to us. If it were not, none of us would be here today.

We have to understand how important we all are. Our ancestors honored us with significance; they sacrificed their quality of life so that we could have a life at all. For it is when we tap into our inner truth, we will create the communities we desire to see. Can we do it? Barack Obama said, "Yes, we can!"

It is no coincidence that good biblical qualities were instilled in us way before we were able to read the pages of the book. Most of us knew it was wrong to steal before we read a word of Genesis. A lot of us have never felt an urge to kill anyone; you can just feel when something is evil and wrong. I know that I loved my neighbor before I knew my ABCs. And since we were made in God's image, the good of God has to be in our DNA.

Oprah Winfrey once said, "Life is a master class. When you learn, teach." And learning from our elders has blessed us with a plethora of wisdom classes; we need to share the lessons of their lives, as our bridge to survive the treacherous waters of America.

It was the American activist and comedy icon Dick Gregory, who said that the two most powerful forces are the black church and the black woman. In reflecting on my southern journey, I could not agree more with the comedic genius. For God's love graced me through my mom.

It takes tons of love to sustain black boys in the South. For in the South we know there are systemic tentacles waiting to latch onto boys that come at us from each direction. These tentacles have only but two purposes. One is to murder our spirits through the miseducation system that feeds us into the criminal justice system. And if those tentacles fail to murder our spirits, their next purpose is to murder us. Rest in power, Ahmaud Arbery.

We have seen many accounts of heavily armed white boys who shoot up movie theaters, Asian massage parlors, or black churches and are arrested without a scratch on them. However, black and brown boys, women, and children are shot, choked, and killed for simply walking unarmed in a park (Rest in Power 12-year-old Tamir Rice).

On top of that, in my home state of Georgia, Governor Brian Kemp, with Ku Klux Klan–like cover under the stillness of a southern morning, signed into law an evil piece of legislation that made it a crime to give water to a citizen who has been forced to stand in intentionally created long voting lines. Just think about how sinister that law is. Let us also analyze what this legislation says about our society.

In 2022, if you give water to an eighty-year-old woman who's been standing patiently in line for two hours waiting to vote, that's a crime. While in South Carolina, a gunman shot nine black people during Bible study, and the police took him to Burger King.

As my pastor says about a thousand times per sermon, "I think I need to say that again!" If grandma is waiting to vote, she cannot have water, but if you are a domestic terrorist who just killed a pastor and eight others, you get to have it your way.

What in the Sam Hell? We need an awakening similar to the Great Awakenings of the 17 and 1800's, when there was an emergence of Protestant pastors singing *Ol' Man River* until our liberation day. We are at our water's edge! In the middle of a pandemic with the waves waiting to crush us on both sides and with the enemy army of racism always barreling at our backs, there is peace beneath the sea.

It is our destiny to cross this River Jordan. At our awakenings inception it is key that we must first have the faith to believe. Our resurrection time is here. But before our awakening can get great—or southern, in this case—allow me to recall some of my first recollections as a child.

My first memory dates to perhaps early 1974. It must have been winter, because I recall walking bare feet across a cold floor and asking my mother, Ida B. Sims, "Ma, how old am I?"

She replied, "You're three."

Also, I remember a time when my father, Roscoe Sims, was looking over my bed rail, proudly admiring his youngest son. I don't recall any events leading up to that father-son moment, and to this day, I'm not certain if that memory was a fleeting moment or if it was all a dream.

But I am certain I could feel the presence, protection, and warmth of God's unconditional love. In my family, my sister, Carol, is the oldest;

she was followed by my brothers, James and Kent, and then me. They were born about a year apart, but I came almost five years after Kent.

At home, the world I was born into was a world shielded by love. For the first five years of my life, our all-black community was down a dirt road. My paternal grandma, Lona Sims, lived less than a quarter mile down the dirt road one way, and my maternal grandma, Big Mama, was about a quarter mile up the road the other way.

Also, I had uncles, aunts, and other relatives insulating my safety, for they too lived along the sides of that dirt road. I have no recollections of the direct encounters I had with racism until I was planted into our school system.

Roscoe, my father, was affectionately called Dust by some of his siblings and relatives. Once I asked my cousin Emma from Ohio, "Why do you call my daddy Dust?"

She said, "When we were children, we would come from Cincinnati to visit Statham, and your daddy would be dusty as smut from working in the fields of red clay."

Often, we overheard elders discussing how young children from that era, all over the South, would be snatched out of school to work in the fields to harvest a white man's crop. I guess black lives didn't matter much then, as evidenced by the South's culture when my father was a child.

Elders too shared stories about how, in the 1940s through the 1960s, our society had little or no intention on educating black and brown children in those times. The theory assumes that it is easier to mislead the masses when they are unlearned. Therefore, there was blatant exploitation of children being snatched out of school and used as an unpaid forced-labor pool. Even the smallest kids were coerced into doing man-sized jobs.

My father's upbringing explained his devotion to hard work. I don't know of a man who worked harder to provide for his family. The system in place at that time intentionally worked black boys so intensely in the fields that they found it difficult to find the time to attend the underfunded Jim Crow schools in the South.

Factoring that with reality leaves little reasoning, but God, to explain my dad's enlightened abilities in mathematics. In just minutes, he could figure out the square footage of complex building plans and determine how much concrete would be required, down to the last rock. Ironically, Rock was my father's other nickname.

Ever since I could remember, my father had a concrete construction company. Roscoe Sims Cement Construction was our family business, and we all played a part. My mother was the records keeper. She paid the bills and taught Carol to keep the records also. At a young age, Carol was responsible for the payroll. She would tabulate the workers' hours and write out all the checks. Those workers were mostly the black men from within our community.

James and Kent worked with our father as well; they both worked like two grown men before either of them reached puberty. Therefore, I guess black lives didn't matter in regards to the child labor laws in our household either.

Anyway, our father was respected throughout our community as well as in our family. He was the seventh of thirteen children of C.L. and Lona Mae Sims—nine boys and four girls.

At first, I wasn't required to work with Dad, as my older brothers did during summers; I had it made in the shade. I would get up late in the day. I would be so deep under the covers that my mother would pretend that she had to dig me out to find me.

After a breakfast of pancakes, eggs, and bacon or a bowl of Lucky Charms, I'd usually go out under the large shady pecan tree to play with my neighbor, Anthony. He and I were almost the same age. And since my father had a construction business, we would play with small cement mixers and dump trucks all day in the dirt. That was so much fun.

Life couldn't get any better on the dirt road, until one day, my brothers bamboozled me. They got out of Dad's truck looking beaten up after a day of laboring in one hundred-degrees of heat.

Then, as if fist-fighting with the southern sun all day wasn't rough enough, they would find me waiting in the shade to give them my best three-minute stand-up comedy routine. For I have always been the family comedian. And my brothers' tattered appearance was my daily source of amusement. I'd go on and on about how tired they looked. I'd say, "Which one of you boys should I call Dusty Rhodes?"

They didn't think I was funny. Nor did they have the energy to invest into any of my foolishness. I looked to Anthony to see if I could get a laugh out of him. "Anthony, don't my brothers look like Pig Pen?" I asked, referring to the kid with a cloud of dust following him in the cartoons *Peanuts* and *Charlie Brown*. Anthony gave me the laugh I was seeking. Later on though, the real joke would be on me.

My brothers and I slept in the same room. That night, they were up talking about how much fun they had working with Dad. My big brothers made work sound so good that they had me believing I was missing out on something as refreshing as a York peppermint patty.

After I had fell face-first into their trap, they convinced me to ask Dad if I could work with him too. I jumped out of the bed and ran into our parents' bedroom in the middle of the night to ask Dad, "Can I go to work with you tomorrow?"

My dad just rolled over and said, "Yeah boy."

When I got back to our room, I didn't even get a chance to share the good news with my brothers; they were already laughing at something or another.

The next day, when I was working in the one hundred-degree heat with the raging southern sun pounding on my face, I realized that my brothers had made a fool out of me.

On the construction site, things moved at a frantic pace. Concrete dries extremely fast in the summer heat, and nobody has the time to train a kid, but I had plenty of questions about the work. Once, my uncle was bent over driving nails into a wooden form board, to hold the concrete in place, and I wanted to ask him about it. I leaned over to ask him a question, and—*wham!*—I was smacked right in the face by his hammer.

My uncle said, "I'm sorry! I didn't see you. Are you alright?"

I said, "Yes Uncle. I'm tough. I'll be fine."

In reality though, I was so traumatized by the up-close and personal encounter with his hammer that I got nervous whenever MC Hammer's music came on decades later in my Uncle Red's night club!

I learned many things by working, and as you just read, I learned some things the hammer hard way. The days were long, and the work was debilitating. When I got home, my neighbor Anthony would be waiting on me to play with the cement mixers, dump trucks, and bulldozers in the dirt under the shade tree, as we used to.

"Hey, Barnard! You want to play with my cement trucks?"

With the little bit of energy I had left, I kicked the toy trucks and bulldozers away and said, "Nah man, this here ain't nothing to play with."

After I started working with Dad, I no longer enjoyed my summer vacations, but I did learn some valuable lessons. I cherish those sacred memories now; for they allowed me to work with my family growing up.

On the other hand, I could never feel much sympathy for Michael Jackson or any of his brothers when they said, "We were forced to work as children." By *work*, Michael and his siblings meant holding microphones to their faces and becoming enormously wealthy, by singing. While in my family, if we had a song to sing, the concrete, the southern sun, and that hammer beat it out of us!

In a sense, the concrete construction industry in the 1970s was similar to the previous generation's cotton industry. My generation in this rural area have stories of working in cement construction just as our parents and grandparents had stories about being cotton sharecroppers.

The big difference was that our ancestors were often cheated out of their earnings at harvest time. And some were even run off their own properties by the evils of some loud and some silent folks. MLK said that in the end, we will remember not the words of our enemies but the silence of our friends.

As a child, I was quiet and shy in public spaces. I hated being forced to give Easter speeches and singing in the choir at my father's home church, Fairfield Missionary Baptist in Statham.

In spite of my apprehensions, every year I was selected to be the king when we went to the Baptist Association.

The association was where the community of churches in our region came together to raise funds for the group, or the association, of churches. And although I never wanted to be the king, I would be selected because my cousin Pearly knew she could depend on me to be there—that is, my parents wouldn't allow me to miss it for the world! It became such a routine that Cousin Pearly wouldn't even ask me if I wanted to be the king that year; she'd just tell my dad what time she'd be picking me up.

Cousin Pearly was also our youth choir director. We had about two good lead singers; and the rest of us were up there in the choir stand rocking the wrong way. At that time, the congregation didn't seem to care that our sound quality wasn't good; they were just glad to see us kids up there rocking the wrong way for the Lord.

Once, Cousin Pearly left the sanctuary for a moment. When she came back, she saw me giving the choir my best imitation of our pastor. Although I am still shy, it is strange how comfortable I have always felt when impersonating someone else.

Let me explain the taboo culture of "playing church," as we still say, to those unfamiliar with that time in the South. We were obsessively superstitious. "Don't step over your brother's back. Spit on the broom if it touches your feet. If a cat crosses in front of your car, put an imaginary X in the corner of the windshield with your finger."

Those superstitions were so imbedded into our subconscious that I recall riding with my Big Ma one day. At the time, she had been senile for years; nonetheless, she still remembered to put an X on our windshield as a cat ran across the road in front of our car.

Furthermore, the worst violation of all the superstitions in our community was imitating or mocking the pastor. In those days, if you did that, you were made to feel as if you were destined for the highway to Hell!

But impersonations were the easiest way for my shy personality to have an outlet. Therefore, the moment Cousin Pearly left the sanctuary, I couldn't help myself, and I crossed the line. I launched into a full sermon, imitating our pastor. I had a handkerchief to continuously keep wiping the sweat off of my forehead.

At the same time, I unceasingly kept folding over the flap of my ear. Somehow, I even managed to get the white foam of spit to cluster in the corners of my mouth. Oh boy, I was preaching and shucking some corn, as we say down South! All the kids in the choir were ecstatically yelling, "Amen!" and "Come on Preacher!"

Just when the spirit got way too high, Cousin Pearly walked back in.

And everyone who was laughing and full of the Holy Ghost went ghost, and the sanctuary fell drop-dead silent. Just as the suspense about how much trouble I was in became unbearable, Cousin Pearly broke out into tears of laughter and said, "Boy you sound just like our pastor! Do it again!"

Of course, I was pleased to oblige her. Ordained by my cousin's encouragement, I really went to shucking some corn then! Oh boy! I certainly had a preponderance of spit pooling in both corners of my mouth, after Pearly gave me her approval. It gave me an indescribable joy to see how my impersonation made her laugh.

Later on, in vacation Bible school (VBS), things got a bit serious again. Our VBS teacher was another cousin, Beatty. Cousin Beatty was a former schoolteacher at the all-black school at the church. On Monday, the first night of VBS, she asked, "How old are you Barnard?"

"I'm twelve," I said.

"That's good. Do you want to join the church?"

"No ma'am, I'm not ready just yet."

Cousin Beatty assured me that it was okay; and that I still had plenty of time to get ready.

My reluctance to join had nothing to do with my love for Christ; it had everything to do with my reluctance on getting my hair wet to be baptized. In those days, wet hair was not an option! There was no way I was going to get my Jheri curl wet. I had waited all my life to get my hair processed. And water—even holy water—is a natural enemy to the Jheri curl.

In defense of my processed hair, let me say that I grew up with two cousins my age who had what we in the black community call "good hair."

When the three of us would be playing together, black adults would say, "Look at those two cute little boys with the curly hair." Adults would leave me out of the cute conversation because of my hair.

You see my Big Ma is part Native American. Thus, some of my relatives had hair flowing like Pocahontas, while I would be sitting there with my hair looking like a Brillo wool scrubbing pad.

Growing up in a culture cultivated in self-hate was already tough. Plus, enduring the daily jokes about my nappy hair as a child was brutal. Therefore, I was not about to mess up my Jheri curl to go back to that life for anybody! I thought that joining the church and accepting Christ would have to wait until the world could accept my nappy hair!

But by that Friday of VBS, the sanctuary seemed as pressurized as a pressure cooker. Cousin Beatty must have realized that she had not met her membership quota. That afternoon, she closed the VBS book and said, "Look outside." We all got up and went to the window. She said, "They say that in the last days, it's going to be extremely hot. Do y'all see all that steam coming off of that pavement?"

We all bucked our eyes and said, "Yes ma'am."

She then turned to me. "Barnard you're twelve, so you're at the age when you need to decide, because you will be held to account for your sins."

As I looked at the steam coming off the pavement, I thought about my impersonation of our pastor. Right as I was pondering that, our pastor came floating into the room!

In that moment, I felt that the timing of his entrance was a direct sign from God. I glanced back at the steam bouncing off the pavement, and a rush of fear overcame me. I ran and jumped into our pastor's arms, almost knocking him down!

Our pastor put me down, grabbed me by my shoulders, and said, "Now wait a minute son! Why do you come?"

I peered back nervously over my shoulders and replied, "Because it's hot outside!"

After that, I joined the church. And I was baptized while wearing a shower cap as if I were swimming in the Olympics for a gold medal. When the pastor reared me back, that doggone shower cap came off and messed up my curls anyway!

By the time we went back into the church for me to take the right hand of fellowship, meaning I was a full-fledged member, my processed hair had dried completely out! There I was in the front of the church, looking like the Cowardly Lion from *The Wizard of Oz*. My Jheri curl was gone, but my natural hair looked just like a lamb's wool.

The self-hate we impose on one another was taught to us by our oppressors. There is no way to look through the historical archives of this nation and to communicate those factual accounts in any white-appeasing way.

There should be no conflating of false equivalencies to confuse the narrative with people-on-both-sides-bear-the-same-blame nonsense. I have asked those who think that way the following questions:

During what time period did black people go out and enslave white people for simply being white? During what era did blacks devise systems to deny white people the right to vote? During which decades did black citizens go out and organize the mass lynching of innocent white citizens?

I have yet to see any references to a time period in which black people came together, in unison, to systematically treat innocent people that way in America. Meanwhile, the evils committed against black people can be counted by the thousands of lifeless bodies recorded by Ida B. Wells-Barnett in her book *The Red Record*. Some may try to misdirect us away from the truth. However, only fools will deny those facts.

Thus, there will be no conflating of false equivalencies in this book. *A Black Man's Guide to Liberating the Rural South* must establish a foundation on truth. The strategy of appeasement allows the murky waters to cloud the white supremacy that surrounds us here every day. Our ancestors' blood stains those waters through no fault of their own. We must call a snake a snake.

As James Baldwin said, the white man's blood that flowed through his veins was not by choice, because his grandmother didn't rape anybody. And we cannot learn from our past if we refuse to face it.

In addition, everyone must understand that not all white people are evil; it's just that those who are wicked in America have been able to take immorality in America to an unfettered and unmatched extreme. Similarly, not all Republicans are racists, but today's Republican Party is a perfect place for racists to hide their ideologies. In 2022, we still have some southern Republicans hollering, "States' rights" as if this were eighteen sixty-two.

It is time for the resurrection, which is the subject of another book I am working on. The resurrection's starting point is a belief that we can revive the rural South. That belief is the first step in owning our personal responsibilities for our communities.

On top of that, we also need to seek political power in our communities by running for local political seats. We are very close, but we could use some of the votes we lost in the great migration to move back south as well. Stacey Abrams has shown us, through organizing, that a red state such as Georgia, can turn blue. The process of our coming of age is what I like to call *The Southern Awakening* from the perspective of *Barnard the Barber*.

Barbers are important pillars in almost every community. Once we utilize the infrastructure of our already established hair care networks, the South will rise again like no one has ever seen!

Seeking solutions unique to our own region doesn't mean we have to see eye to eye on methods. Seeking solutions simply means that we are respecting that we all have eyes. Our eyes are the windows to our souls. Your soul is what you must search to make our society better. Dr. King said, "We must live together as brothers or perish together as fools."

Me opening up to write this book is just a testament acknowledging that I too still have work to do. I once was blind, but now I see. I too am American. Meaning we all have value, and we all can contribute to the great cause to liberate marginalized people.

For instance, if we know two angles of a triangle, together we can easily figure out the measurement of the third. All we need to do is just add the measurements of the first two angles and subtract that total from 180 to get the measurement of the third.

Figuring out the measurement of the third angle with this formula is easy, if we are humble enough to accept the measurements of the first two angles. Some solutions are really that simple.

Although, some of our societal solutions seem impossible because we are constantly having to spend so much time and energy convincing some adults that the three-sided shape is a triangle! One cannot know all the answers, but with an open mind full of humility, we can at least all learn our shapes.

Once I was in a studio, trying to learn how to record music, with Lester Troutman Sr. from the world-renowned Zapp Band. He asked me right off, before we pushed one button, "Barnard, are you inquisitive?"

"What the heck does *inquisitive* mean?" I asked.

He laughed and said, "Brother Barnard, I think you're going to be okay."

And so will you. May all our powers engage!

Postulate 1

THE SOUTH HAS SOMETHING TO SAY!

THE SOUTHERN AWAKENING is a coming-of-age experience for people in the rural South. In the awakening's beginning, the word is "The South has something to say." In this book, you will hear the word not from Andre 3000 but from me, Barnard the Barber. Barbers and beauticians are uniquely privileged to have a hand on the pulse of their communities. And I have had my hand on my community's pulse ever since I was fourteen.

With over thirty-six years of experience in the field of barbering, I know for sure that listening is the critical key. For instance, would you go back to a barber or hairstylist who never listened to your requests? In barbering, I have learned to listen before I open my mouth. I've learned to do that in hopes that when I do speak, my prayer is that I will have something enlightening to say.

My style of communicating is direct so that we don't miss the point. Understanding that we cannot tiptoe through the tulips with the challenges we face in communities all across the South. No one would expect a medical doctor to sugarcoat negative test results. Think about that for a moment? What good is a doctor who would say to me, "Barnard, your BMI is over thirty percent. That's obese? Just keep up the good work overeating". While a doctor's bad recommendations could be deadly, we must also communicate in truth to shed our lives societal shackles.

Also, my style is to communicate harsh truths in a comical way. This book suggestively outlines and gives actionable steps for communities to progress in this day and time. Being together in truth and love is the only way we can reach our goals.

Fairness and equality make up a love sandwich.

Also, as a school of thought, I do not feel the need of conforming to the European standards of enlightenment as most of my fellow African Americans descendants around me have. To free and non-assimilating minds, the truth does not require a stamp of any man's approval to be perceived as validated.

Therefore, it is always my humble attempt to communicate in simple southern words. Meaning again, I don't feel the normal pressures to conform to European standards by pretending to be a professor at some prestigious college.

My writing style is in essence, coming from a core spiritual source. Evolving from an understanding that in African culture, the wisest person in the village is usually the one who has spent the most time absorbing the wisdom passed down from the elders. Being the barber in our village has blessed me with countless of hours to listen and to learn from the descendants of my African-American village.

When I was a small kid, my mom would fill the floor up with blank pieces of paper and encourage me to draw for hours. Sometimes I would start a sketch with no idea of what I was aiming to draw. Creativity would flow through me, from untapped reserves that I never even knew existed.

Years later, I took a literature night class at Athens Technical College. The professor taught the same class at the University of Georgia during the day. She introduced us to Richard Wright, James Baldwin, and Langston Hughes.

In one of our night classes, I read that thoughts were like seeds: when planted, cultivated, and nourished, they could blossom into beautiful blooms. Our professor kicked the gate open for me in a session of free writing; for an entire class, we'd sit there writing with no preconceptions of what we'd write about.

That took me back to my days of drawing and creating on blank pieces of paper on my mother's floor to see what the source could stream through me. Free writing is just painting with words. *The Southern Awakening* is my humble offering in that vein. I'm just the little drummer boy whose sticks are these words.

Any wisdom that you might hear is a gift from God that's being allocated through me because I humbly listened to the wisdom of elders, parents, siblings, children, uncles, aunts, friends, and clients over the years. Now that doesn't mean I think that everything I've learned was always right. (I will get deeper into that conversation in postulate 5, "A Customer Is Not Always Right.")

Nevertheless, barbershops are meccas of information for our communities when we utilize the tools of discernment. Discernment helps us to identify when we are heading in the right direction. Discernment also teaches us to quickly recognize when we are headed the wrong way.

Some of these stories in this book are inspired writings sourced from a love of listening and an untainted passion to share what I've learned. Again, as Oprah said, life is a master class, and when you learn, you teach. This project and my next book, *The Resurrection*, were lessons scribbled down in the chaos of COVID-19.

Our barbershop was closed due to the pandemic. Our schools were closed as well; my children were doing virtual learning at home. Once I believed I was good in math, or at least that's what my teacher told me.

Therefore, I figured I could help our youngest with her math. *For Pete's sake*, I thought, *it's only third-grade stuff. I might as well show this teacher what I know.* I found out the hard way that these kids are way smarter than I am. Also, I saw firsthand that our teachers are phenomenal, and they were especially spectacular throughout this crisis, specifically in the way they dealt with virtual parents like me.

Our daughter's teacher had to spend more time working with me than the other kids in her class. I was stacking numbers and carrying the ones like we did in the Stone Ages, but the teacher wanted us to group the larger numbers first. She tried to explain to me that the new way of processing numbers was more efficient.

"Mr. Barnard," she said, "we have switched to a cognitively guided learning system nowadays." That lady told me that as if I was supposed to know what the heck a cognitively guided learning system was!

I passed the third grade many moons ago, but I would have been held back this time if I had not dropped out and quit as a grown man!

For that reason, I found it wiser to leave our children's schooling to the experts. After the hand of wisdom snatched me out of my virtual third grade cubicle, I am now the silent virtual dad listening from way off on the side.

Still though being a supportive dad on the side, I was afforded the special opportunity to reflect and write down some of what I'd learned over the years as a barber. From that journey, the free writing became a rainbow in the cloud now called *The Southern Awakening*.

The South can and will rise again, but this time, we will make the South rise in the right way. There is no need to reinvent the wheel here. This is not a book claiming to create solutions from out of the thin southern air. This book's origin came from studying what our ancestors did during the Reconstruction era to empower blacks all across the South.

Black Wall Streets were created because black people were forced to shop with and depend on one another for goods and services. During the Reconstruction Era in the late 1800s, the South was actually making America great in terms of our economic sustainability.

We were doing surprisingly well on our own in our communities before rural towns were trampled by the feet of terrorism and white supremacy. Back then, we actually had more blacks serving as senators than we do now. Hiram Revels became the first African American senator of Mississippi in 1870, and just last year, Raphael Warnock became the first African American senator from Georgia in 2021.

Which means we are on the cusp of something amazing right here and now. We can allow the ropes of our past to hold us back like strange fruit, or we can whip that rope forward like Stacey Abrams and lasso it to the shining stars. If we look up, we have the stars as our guiding light to our bright future. As always, in our quest, we must anticipate resistance.

So, hold on tight for the bumpy ride. Our history has taught us that power will concede nothing without a struggle. Yet still, we can get our communities to where we want them to be. We don't need another insurrection. What we do need is a resurrection—one of the best kinds. As barbers and beauticians, we are the glue that connects people from all walks of life. It is time that we tap into the accessible power of our connections.

In the activist training classes I took, the speaker told us that when we were doing our jobs well, people on both sides would hate to see us coming. I knew from my training that I had been validated as an activist in our town when I couldn't even get a volunteer job coaching Statham Little League baseball.

One morning, I was driving to work and I saw what seemed to be hundreds of "We Need Volunteer Coaches" signs at every turn. I thought they were signs from God intentionally meant for me. When I walked in to volunteer at Statham First Baptist Church in 2014, a hush went through the white congregants in the room.

As I carefully scanned the characters demeanor, I hesitantly approached the lady at the check-in desk. An older woman had a stack of papers for volunteer registrations. I politely asked, "Ma'am, is this where I can sign up as a volunteer coach?" She looked at me and said that they were no longer accepting registrations; because all the coaching positions had already been filled.

This was a shock because I had just seen the signs asking for volunteers. Disappointed, I glanced at the lonely blank registration papers all crying out for a coach's help. But according to her, there was no room in the inn for me. As a southern gentleman, I simply said, "Thank you," to the woman and politely went on to work.

My first client always came by the salon on his days off. He was a friend we called Bowling Ball. I told him about being denied a volunteer coaching position. Bowling Ball laughed and replied the way Smokey, Chris Tucker's character in the movie *Friday*, says, "Dang it, man! How do you get fired on your day off?" Except in my situation, Bowling Ball said, "Dang it, man! How do you not get hired for a volunteer position?"

Usually I was the one serving up the jokes. I felt a bit hurt about being denied the position, but at least he was amused. Bowling Ball could see the grief on my face, because he tried to brighten me up by saying, "You know what, B? I'll go over there and sign up to see if they will let me coach, and then I'll get you to help me." I told him that sounded like a plan.

Bowling went to the same cold church and asked the same older woman about volunteering as a coach. He told me she warmly welcomed him with open arms and quickly handed him one of the lonely registration forms.

Bowling signed up, and she thanked him for being willing to be a coach. She asked him if he would recruit more coaches, because they really needed some more help. Bowling replied, "Yeah. I'm going to get Barnard the Barber to come help me out."

With the fierce urgency of now, the church lady snatched the registration form from Bowling's loving hands. After tearing Bowling Ball's filled-out form in half, she said, "I'm sorry, but we don't need any coaches like that over here."

Bowling came back to the salon with his head held down, he was feeling mighty low. I asked, "What happened?"

He replied, "B, you got me fired from a volunteer position on my day off."

Some people in the South only like shrinking Negros. If you are black in the south, and no one ever has any issues with you here, it is probably because you have mastered becoming the shrinking Negro that some folks adore.

On the other hand, if you're challenging the status quo, it is unreasonable to expect every single person to like you all of the time.

Although, if you are accepted by everyone in the South, it's probably because you have unconsciously mastered the art of shrinking to fit into the spaces that those with a superiority complex are comfortable with seeing you in. I hear all the time from shrinking Negroes, "Barnard, I've been one of the few blacks working here for thirteen years, and I have never seen any racial issues."

The fact that an employee can comfortably say that, "I am one of the few blacks working here," is the first sign that there are racial issues all around. When I ask, "How many raises or promotions have you received in your thirteen years of faithful service?"

The typical response is "Not a one." Therefore, the reason black folks who work in these environments don't see inequities is not because there aren't any inequities present. This type of Negro has grown accustomed to go day after day pretending not to see injustice just to get by.

The good Negroes, as we call them also, get used to shrinking for white folks by not challenging the racial disparities, even when those disparities are spitting them in their faces every day.

While in my home, I learned that it is not ever my job to shrink to fit in. Many days, before I left our house, my mother would grab me by my face, look me square in my eyes, and say, "Son, you aren't any better than anybody, but you definitely ain't no less than anybody either!" What I took that to mean was "Don't you dare shrink yourself just to fit in."

Although we know the Reverend Dr. Martin Luther King is celebrated now, but while he was alive, many black churches in the South didn't want him in their pulpits. This was because non-shrinking activists who call out problems are blamed for causing the problems they call out.

The attitude of black churches in the South, with the world on fire around them was "We don't need Dr. King down here causing all these problems." But in reality, it wasn't King who bombed the Sixteenth Street Baptist Church; In opposition, King was actually the one who called the bombing one of the most vicious and tragic crimes against humanity.

The sad irony is the fact that the Klansmen who stuck nineteen sticks of dynamite in that church and killed four little girls, they weren't the ones who had to write a letter from the Birmingham jail. But Martin Luther King Jr. did! Calling out terrorism is not what cultivates our culture to recreate environments for these criminal murderous acts.

When in actuality, honestly admitting that there is a problem is the first step to finding solutions.

King wasn't born until 1929 in Atlanta. While the Atlanta massacre happened in 1906. This massacre in which ninety African Americans and ten whites were injured or killed, predated King's birth by twenty-three years. Therefore, how could anyone conclude that King caused that racial riot or America's racial tensions?

Accordingly, if your doctor tells you that you have high cholesterol, that doesn't mean the doctor caused it. The doctor didn't make you eat that fatback with fried chicken and gravy; the doctor just analyzed the detrimental data. Dr. King was only reporting the facts about our nation that the six o'clock news would not.

Today, Al Sharpton comes to lend his powerful voice and to render aid and comfort to families who need to know that someone cares. The good Reverend has never shot anybody or kept his knee on a man's neck for more than nine minutes. Reverend Al is like the ambulance coming to lend a helping hand to our communities in times of crisis. We have to get the language right, if we expect to be on the right side of making history. The elements of truth in itself is transformational!

During the pandemic, while meditating and self-reflecting, I realized that the resurrection should always start with me working on bettering me. Historically, movements that have transcended our nation have often started in a small olive-branch church or a barbershop somewhere anyway, right? *The Southern Awakening* is my humble offering to shine a light on these remote places, to unite and empower the entire southern region.

Postulate 2

REIMAGINE AND RESEARCH TO REINVENT SELF-SUSTAINABLE COMMUNITIES

REIMAGINING DOESN'T MEAN we have to invent solutions. We only need to do the research to become the bridges between the wisdom of our ancestors and our youth today. Once we are able to connect those critical dots of possibilities, we are destined to see the South reemerge as the political and economic force it has always had the potential to be.

In the years following Reconstruction, some black folks in the South were actually doing well financially, despite the Jim Crow laws that relegated people of color to second-class citizenship. Because our predecessors weren't allowed to patronize some white businesses, they were forced to spend their dollars in their own communities. Segregation obligated us to practice collective economics, which I will discuss in a later chapter of this book.

Due to collective economics, many black-owned businesses were doing remarkably well—that is until white terrorism raged and flowed through rural townships all across the South. The more I learn about the Reconstruction Era, the more I learn that white terrorism didn't destroy just one Black Wall Street.

White folks all over lost their minds in the presence of well-to-do black and brown people. White anxiety is created from just seeing

Negroes living in peace, and those angst still causes a many white folks to blow a fuse today. James Baldwin was asked once, "What does the Negro really want in America?"

His response was "The Negro just wants to be left alone." What Baldwin understood was that black people are resilient when they were not terrorized and subjected to unequal treatment under the law. Historically we have proven that we can do anything anybody else can, and sometimes we can do it far better. Although most of the times, it seems as if everyone around us knows this truth except us.

Through research I was led right to my very own relative. Asbury McClusky owned an enormous amount of land off of Highway 53, at the intersection of Barrow, Oconee, and Walton counties in the 1920s. Asbury McClusky was a brilliant farmer who owned more than 380 acres, which is almost four times as much land as Disneyland in California and nearly a hundred acres more land than Six Flags over Georgia.

McClusky was so wealthy that he had to put his money in separate banks. He had to hide his hard-earned money so as not to trigger envious white rage. That rage is the source of southern rule number one (which I will discuss in postulate 6).

Even though Asbury could afford a new car, he drove his horse and wagon into town to be modest and in an effort not to piss the white folks off.

McClusky would buy extra food to give to his white neighbors when they fell on hard times. In spite of all his efforts to appease his white neighbors, they turned into domestic terrorists simply because McClusky wanted to help his black neighbors as well. Isn't it funny how some white people are cool with the idea of black-on-black crime but fly into a frenzied rage at the idea of black-on-black empowerment?

While pondering that, in the middle of the night, a group of daytime neighbors turned into nighttime knights' men of the Ku Klutz Klan. The mob broke into Asbury's house with guns blazing. Although injured, McClusky somehow got his wife and kids to safety. McClusky managed to hold the terrorist off with return gunfire as he escaped into the night to go into protective custody in Atlanta.

The Klansmen were so mad that they hadn't killed Asbury that they came back and made similar attacks on his black neighbors, Will and his pregnant wife, Odessa Peters. Will was also able to hold the Klansmen off until he could escape into protective custody in Atlanta as well.

After the attack, the group of white savages got hold of his pregnant wife and beat her mercilessly. As if that weren't cruel and inhumane enough, the domestic terrorism continued on into the courtroom by means of legislative lawlessness: the white judges and lawyers brutalized the law to "legally" steal the Peters family's land!

These incidents were not isolated in the South. Some are documented in books, including *The Seeds of Southern Change: The Life of Will Alexander* and *Born to Rebel* by Benjamin E. Mays, former president of Morehouse College.

Such terrorism provided a platform for understanding this curse of fear that has been passed down through many generations of black families. Putting these pages back into our history helps us to understand how blacks were robbed of their ability to pass on their hard-earned generational wealth.

These incidents and many other similar tragedies happened not that many years ago. I point this out because some like to think that injustice ended when slavery was "legislatively" abolished, but it still touches and negatively affects us from an economic standpoint today. The law doesn't change minds when it's hiring time.

When my father had his cement business, we worked with other black-owned cement companies too. If we had a huge job, we would contact other cement contractors to help us out.

We most often teamed up with our cousin Milton's crew. He and my father were double cousins—my grandmother Lona Stroud (Sims) and Milton's mother, Zona Stroud (Sims), were sisters, and my grandfather C.L. Sims and Milton's father were first cousins. As kids, we were fascinated with wrestling. We all thought Cousin Milton looked like one of the few black wrestlers in the 1970s, Ernie Ladd.

One day I tied a bath towel around my neck, pretending to fly around like a superhero. Cousin Milton yelled, "I see you Superman!"

I responded, "Cousin Milton, I'm not Superman! Can't you tell I'm Shazam?"

"Oh, I see you, Shazam!" he said.

And almost fifty years later, until he transitioned, my dear Cousin Milton still called me Shazam.

In those days, we also loved to watch TV shows. As a family, we ate dinner together every night and then watched *Good Times*, *The Jeffersons*, *Dallas*, and *The Dukes of Hazzard*, among other favorites. Even though *Good Times* and *The Jeffersons* were set in the big city, our family could relate to their characters. Seeing black families on TV in those times was rare.

Seeing strong black men, such as James Evans and George Jefferson, was relatable to us because my father was the strong lead man in our home. George Jefferson even had his own business, as my dad did. JJ was the funny guy and the artist on the show, and I related to him because I enjoyed making my siblings laugh as well.

And then there was Thelma on *Good Times*—as James Brown would say, "Good God!"—her boundless beauty would stop the story line of any episode the moment she entered a scene. Thelma was the standard of beauty, much like my sister Carol is today.

As children, in our home we were only taught about our human connections. Therefore, it was easy for us to identify with the characters the in all-white TV shows as well. We loved to watch *Dallas* and *The Dukes of Hazzard*, too.

On *Dallas*, the Ewings were brothers who worked in their family's oil business, just as my family all worked in our dad's concrete business. *Dallas*'s J.R. Ewing and my oldest brother, J.R., had the same initials, but that was where my brother's similarities to the ruthless J.R. Ewing's character ended.

We also shared a close human connection with the *Dukes of Hazzard* family because the scenery was just like where we lived. Two white boys flying up and down dirt roads in the South while being chased by Sheriff Roscoe P. Coltrane was right up our alley. You see in our minds, it correlated to our story well because our alleys were one-lane dirt roads, and our sheriff's name was Roscoe too.

We would fly up and down our dirt roads like Bo and Luke Duke, trying to make our hair blow in the wind like the Duke boys'. My brother Kent and I nearly ran off the bridge across the creek while trying to go fast enough to get our hair to move like the good ole boys'! We had the windows of our Buick down as we sped down the dirt road at about 102 miles per hour, but still, we couldn't get our tiny Afros to move like the good ole boys' hair did.

We had some kind of imagination to believe our Buick sedan was the Dukes' 1969 Dodge Charger, which they named after General Robert E. Lee. At the time, we didn't understand who General Lee was, and I didn't understand what the Confederate flag on the roof of the Duke boys' car meant.

One time, I went shopping with my mother, and we stopped at a town store called Roses. Roses sold all sorts of things, but for me, the main attraction was always the toy section. My mother always did the black mom's speech before we entered any store: "You don't see nothing. You don't want nothing. And don't you ask for nothing. Do you understand me?"

I would say, "Yes ma'am," but there was always some toy in the store that would start calling my name.

On one particular day, I saw exactly what I needed: A *Dukes of Hazzard* wallet decorated with the Confederate flag. I went to my mom with the wallet I just had to have. I started begging like Keith Sweat: "Mama, please! Don't say no! I need this wallet more than old folks need soft shoes."

My mama looked at that wallet with the Confederate flag on it, then she looked at me, and said, "Boy, I am not buying you no mess like this!"

"But, Ma, it's *The Dukes of Hazzard*!"

At only about nine years old, my mother knew that I had no idea what that flag stood for. She asked, "What do you need a wallet for anyway? You don't have any money to put in it."

"This summer, when I go to work with Daddy, I'll make some money, and then I'll have a good place to keep it." I said

Who knows if it was the begging like Keith Sweat or if it was the proposal I made about saving money, but one of the two got my mom to give in and buy me that wallet! I must have pulled that wallet out of my pocket a thousand times a day.

I wanted everyone to see my billfold, as we called them back then. Strangely, no one made fun of my billfold until I took it to school. The only kids who got a good laugh about my wallet were white.

It was as if the white kids knew what that flag meant, but their parents still pretended not to. My good friend Rex saw me flexing my wallet and asked, "Man, what are you doing with that?" He knew exactly what the flag meant; one flew near his home. He and the other white kids laughed at my wallet every time I took it out of my pocket. I pulled my wallet out so many times that the flag began to fade by the end of the day.

Nowadays, with smartphones and the internet, every person should know what that flag means. Yet and still, in the South, we have many grown men riding around looking as silly as I did in the third grade. Similarly, we also have monuments erected all over the South by the Daughters of the Confederacy.

Those girls did a number on history by sensationalizing the legacy of white supremacy. It is no wonder so many have forgotten the flag's initial purpose. Let's also not forget the Confederate flag's timely resurgence was when Jim Crow laws were being struck down as unconstitutional by the master attorney and eventual Supreme Court Justice Thurgood Marshall.

The call for states' rights also emerged around the same time as the Confederacy was branded into Georgia's state flag in 1956, only two years after *Brown vs the Board of Education* in 1954.

Regarding the Confederate flag's origins, designer William Thompson didn't like a previous Confederate flag design because he said it looked too much like the flag of the United States of America. Imagine if we could have taught that fact to kids? Maybe those kids wouldn't have grown up to become worshipers of the Confederate flag, while complaining that they think that Colin Kaepernick is the one who is disrespecting the American flag. Talk about a hypocritical contradiction in regards to patriotism!

In addition, we need to know that William Thompson's stated purpose for designing the Confederate flag was this: "We are fighting to maintain the heaven-ordained supremacy of the white man over the inferior or colored race."

Yet years later, the people I see at the corner store will still try to convince me the Confederate flag means something different from what the flag's creator intended it to mean. That's like me trying to teach them that the middle finger really means "Have a nice day!" In this scenario, reimagining does mean reinventing. The Daughters of the Confederacy rewrote our history to favor the treasonous sons, of our founding fathers.

Our mother was the next-to-youngest daughter in her family. She was one of nine; two baby girls died within a year of birth. Both of my parents and all of their siblings were born at home and/or with a midwife due to blacks not being allowed in hospitals or safer health care facilities.

My mother's parents were John Calvin Muckle and Lona Lee (Moon) Muckle. Our maternal grandparents were affectionately called Big Mama and Big Daddy. Our calling our grandmother Big Mama had nothing to do with her size. I was only about eight when I noticed that I was taller than she was. I would walk up to Big Mama to make sure she noticed I was taller than her too. I said, "Big Mama, I'm taller than you."

Big Mama said, "Yeah, but I'll still beat your tail!"

My mother laughed because she remembered her older brother, Joe Charles Muckle, the sibling closest to my mother in age, walking up to Big Mama when they were young and being told the same thing. I never heard Big Mama talk about her youngest son much at all.

Uncle Joe was somewhat of a mystery for me then. As children, my siblings and I never knew what happened to him. Whenever we sat around listening to our elders talk of old times, the casual mention of Uncle Joe's name brought the conversation to a screeching halt.

Much later in life, I would grow to understand more about the psychological effects that tragedies can have on families from one generation to the next. The ecosystem of trauma flows through black families, as Ambassador Andrew Young explained, goes a little something like this.

A black man goes out into the world, and the world treats him badly. In turn, the black man comes home and treats his wife poorly. The mom takes out her frustrations on her children. The kids kick the dog. The dog chases the cat, and by that time, poor Mickey Mouse doesn't stand a chance! In the words of Erykah Badu, this cycle goes on and on, and on and on.

The post-traumatic effects of being targeted causes rippling waves across our culture. The killing of my uncle Joe sounds similar to the police execution of eighteen-year-young Michael Brown in Ferguson, Missouri, on August 9, 2014.

On October 6, 1963, Uncle Joe was driving on a back road in Barrow County, Georgia, with a friend I'll call Jane. According to her firsthand account, a Barrow County deputy's car with officers Yearwood and Fagan and two other self-deputized white male vigilantes were riding in the back of the police car that stopped my twenty-three-year-old uncle Joe.

For reasons I have yet to have explained, Officer Yearwood or Officer Fagan put my uncle in handcuffs, arrested him, and placed him in the center of the backseat of the police car. Jane told us the other two vigilantes were sitting on either side of my handcuffed uncle as the police car left Jane alone on the rural roadside. Mind you that all this was after, what we were told was a routine traffic stop.

Later, my oldest uncle, Johnny, a Korean War veteran and an NAACP president at one time, told me Joe, his younger brother, was said to have magically escaped his handcuffs like Houdini and somehow stopped the police cruiser from the backseat of the car.

I can't figure out how that could have happened. Uncle Joe was a small man who supposedly pushed his way out of the backseat of the car, from between two large sized vigilantes and ran off into the woods.

Then the two officers and the two vigilantes chased after uncle Joe. While running away for his life, Uncle Joe supposedly picked up a stick, and turned back to pursue the four white men who were chasing him with guns!

Yet Officer Fagan was said to have somehow shot my charging uncle in the back of his head. Could you explain all of these conflicting occurrences to a grieving family with a straight face?

How can one man escape handcuffs and a police car, whose back doors only opened from the outside of the car, still get away with four gun bearing vigilantes surrounding him?

Then the four lawless vigilantes would have to believe that this unarmed escape artist somehow got a gun from the thin southern air, just in time to charge at them with a stick. You tell me, what good is a stick at a gun fight? Furthermore, how can a charging man be shot in the back of the head?

Let's face it the movie *The Matrix* doesn't have half of the special effects of these lies we were told. There is a long history of police reports that make up inconceivable stories, just to cover up criminal police misconduct.

Black communities are numb from hearing about citizen and police encounters that are illogical and impossible to believe. The 2014 case when eighteen-year-old Mike Brown was killed in Ferguson, Missouri, reminded us of what happened to Uncle Joe.

Officer Darren Wilson too claimed that a bare-handed black boy charged into his barrage of bullets. That is as strange as "Strange Fruit." I have never met a bullet proof black boy yet, have you?

Those unanswered details about my uncle Joe Charles's death weighed on Uncle Johnny's heart heavily. The killing of his youngest brother kept him up late at night for the rest of his life. He told me the trauma of that experience inspired him to become an activist in the NAACP. He was a Korean War veteran, but the racial war in America is the battle that put the most severe scars on his soul.

Uncle Johnny said he went to war for his country over in Korea only to come back and see his baby brother killed right here in the good ole USA.

He bunked with white soldiers in Korea. He was treated as if they were all brothers in Korea, because the soldiers' lives depended on their brotherhood. However, the moment Uncle Johnny planted his feet back on American soil, the brotherhood dissolved.

You see America's soil is so toxic with racism that honorable brothers can become like Cain and Abel. Racist toxicity can penetrate a soldier's boots in the instant their feet touches our fertile grounds. With tears in his eyes, Sergeant Johnny Muckle shared with me that one of the white soldiers he had bunked with for years said to him as their ship was about to dock, "Well, Sergeant Muckle, I guess it's back to being a nigger for you again."

The national anthem sounds for many blacks in America like "O say can you see why the dawn, feels like night?"

It is as if America the beautiful is in a marathon of Wrestle Manias, trying to rectify her issues with race. My paternal grandma loved to watch wrestling. She would sit in front of her TV, dipping snuff and arguing with the wrestlers on TV as if they could hear her.

"Don't you hit Dusty Rhodes in the back with that chair now Ric Flair! Watch out now! Here comes that crazy fool the Sheik!" We would all scream along with her as we watched. No one could have told any of us that wrestling wasn't real in those days.

In fact, years later, I met the Iron Sheik at a club called Toppers in Athens, Georgia, where the club's promotion was wrestling night. I was nervous to approach the Iron Sheik, because I confused the Iron Sheik with the original Sheik, who ate fire and licked snakes. The Iron Sheik was nothing like the bizarre Sheik we were used to seeing on TV while watching wrestling with our grandma.

I talked with the Sheik for a couple of hours and found him to be a sound and reasonable guy. During our conversation, I told the Iron Sheik how big a fan my grandmother was, and he said, "I live in Gainesville, Georgia. That's not too far from where your grandmother lives in Statham. I'll give you my number. Call me if she wants me to stop by to see her." Then he gave me an autographed photo of himself and signed it to my grandma Lona Mae Sims.

The next day, I took the photo to Grandma and said, "Grandma, the Sheik said he wants to come by to see you."

Grandma's eyes got really big. "Lord no! I don't need that fool over hear breaking chairs, licking snakes, and spitting out flames! Oh no! No, thank you! This photo of that fool is close enough for me. Tell the Sheik thank you though baby."

Though wrestling might not be real, the racism my precious grandmother suffered through is as real as it gets.

My grandma told me in her day, she could pick more cotton than any man; we often talked a lot about the circumstances and conditions in the South. However, my grandma had two brothers whom I never heard her mention: William and Sterling Stroud, affectionately called Bub and Shine.

The two boys, around twelve and fourteen, just went missing into the thin southern air one day. None of us know exactly what happened to them, and in those days, black people were understandably too terrorized to keep asking.

As a survival mechanism, my poor grandma, as a little girl, had to suppress the grief of losing two brothers in silence. Until this very day, all we can do is wonder what happened to my great-uncles Bub and Shine.

Although we all have our suspicions, based on the same culture that killed fourteen-year-old Emmett Till. We still have questions, yet generations have passed down the tradition of surviving by remaining too afraid to ask. One must come to realize that it takes true closure to properly heal a wound. And we cannot heal right until we get the answers any loved one deserves.

As if living through that weren't enough, my dear grandma's next-to-oldest son, Willie West Sims, died tragically in the southern summer of 1985. Two respected citizens of Barrow County were left dead, also leaving us with more questions than answers.

Uncle Willie West was also a Korean War veteran. I never had the chance to ask him much about his experiences in serving our country as a soldier; I only knew him as a tall, handsome man who loved gardening and riding his Massey Ferguson tractor. Uncle Willie West was an excellent mechanic who worked at a shop in town.

He fixed my go-kart for me by adjusting the governor; to make it go a little faster than it was supposed to. After I wrecked my go-kart while trying to be the black Evel Knievel in attempting to jump over my Statham version of the Grand Canyon, he put my go-cart back together for me again. Seeing that my career as the next Evel Knievel might be cut short, Uncle West bought me an Etch-A-Sketch for Christmas because he knew I also loved to draw.

On a hot summer day, as Uncle West was getting off work, I was told, a white woman's car broke down in front of the mechanic shop where he worked. Being a southern gentleman and a seasoned mechanic, he fixed the lady's car, saving her from being stranded on the side of the road.

Then Mr. Barnett, a white man who owned the gas station across the street, saw them talking and got the wrong impression. Triggered by the mere sight, Barnett ran up to Uncle West threatening him with something in his hand.

We may never know all the particulars of what happened next, but I do know it's unrealistic to train a man to go to war in a foreign land, and then expect him not to be able to defend his own manhood here at home.

Every man is supposed to have a right to stand his ground, especially in the South, right? That is not the way it has historically worked for people of color around here; even tall and handsome black men are expected to shrink in the south. But most grown men will get tired of shrinking. The details leading up to what happened next are debatable, but what happened later was irrefutable.

Uncle Willie ended up shooting Barnett in the middle of town. Our school bus rode right by Barnett's dead body lying in a pool of his own blood. How we all wished that Barnett's and Uncle West's trains didn't collide on that tragic day.

Uncle West turned himself in to the police and was later found hanged in his cell. Not many people believe he took his own life. The KKK was said to have gathered in front of the jail the night my uncle supposedly hung himself.

In the South, we still have authorities who will make up impossible things, such as saying seventeen-year-young Kendrick Johnson rolled himself up in a wrestling mat and died at school in Valdosta, Georgia, on January 10, 2013.

My uncle Willie West's tragedy also reminds me of Sam Hose, a friendly, skilled, and intelligent worker in Coweta, Georgia. On April 12, 1899, he was said to have been threatened by his white employer simply for requesting time off to visit his sick mother.

His employer, Alfred Cantor, pointed a gun at Sam, threatening to kill him, and Sam threw an ax at Cantor, striking and killing him in self-defense. To intensify the rage directed at Sam, additional lies were added to the account. Bonus lies circulated claiming that Cantor's white wife had been raped as well, though she said those accusations were false. Can you imagine that—an imagined rape of a white woman in the rural South?

Sam Hose's case never made it to trial; southern justice didn't work that way. A lynch mob of nearly two thousand terrorists took Hose from the courthouse to a patch of land known as the Old Troutman Field.

News reports wrote that the mob cut off Hose's ears, fingers, and genitals. He was then chained to a Georgia pine, and the skin was peeled off his face. While Sam was still screaming, a torturous terrorist pierced him in the side. The white mob then doused Sam with kerosene and burned him alive.

A journalist documented that the pain Hose had endured was so intense that his veins ruptured, and his eyes nearly burst from their sockets. Another journalist recorded that the mob watched with satisfaction as Hose's body contorted as he screamed in pain.

One woman thanked God for the great job the extremists did in inflicting so much pain on Hose. Many spectators reported hearing Hose yelling and screaming, "Oh my God! Oh Jesus!" His heavenly cries were heard yet no earthly human offered Hose any help.

Author, scholar, and noted civil rights leader W.E.B. DuBois lived in nearby Atlanta at the time. He was on his way to a meeting with the *Atlanta Constitution* in an attempt to appeal to our nation's moral senses about the horrors of lynching in America.

On the way to that meeting, DuBois saw that Hose's body parts were being sold at a market on the road he was walking on—his liver, his knuckles, and other parts of his corpse were for sale as keepsakes.

Alarmed at the sight, Dubois the intellectual canceled his meeting because he no longer believed he could rationalize morals to people who could proudly display such savagery. My guess is Dubois concluded that there was no use in trying to speak peace to American maniacs.

Tragically, we never learned about these historical accounts in school. Children should, because the best way to be better is to learn from our past mistakes. Thank God for the songwriters who see the value in telling our stories through song, because as Marvin Gaye sang, "Make me wanna holler, the way they do my life!"

In my life, I have no memories of either of my grandfathers because they both died by the time I was two. My mother said I would be waiting for my older siblings to get home from school, and my Big Daddy would stop by because he saw me waiting at our front door. Big Daddy entertained me as I waited by picking me up high over his head.

Those exciting encounters filled the voids of time. There was no prekindergarten education when I was a child. My Pre-K consisted of things I learned from my older siblings and the daily doses of *Sesame Street*. I loved that show so much that when my sister, Carol, called me Kermit the Frog, I still take it as a compliment.

My sister was referring to the size of my bulging eyes in proportion to my head at the time. That never bothered me, because I was a huge fan of Kermit then, and it doesn't bother me now when she still calls me that today.

Sesame Street had a big effect on me in a way I probably took for granted before my formal schooling began. *Sesame Street* gave me a daily depiction of diversity. Ernie and Bert were yellow and brown, Super Grover was blue, and Snuffleupagus's eyelashes were on fleek! Then there was the beautiful Maria, who exposed a country kid like me to Spanish. Maria was very pretty, and I learned to count in Spanish before I knew how to count in English.

I read the following in a July 26, 2021, ParentCo. blog:

> Studies by Harvard University confirm that the creativity, critical thinking skills, and flexibility of the mind are significantly enhanced if children learn a second language at a younger age. Preschool years, especially the first three years of life, are believed to be a vital period in a child's life. This is when the foundations for attitudes, thinking, and learning, among others, are laid down.

This is why I credit having those daily doses of diversity for giving me an appreciation for other cultures. If there was no *Sesame Street,* my vision of the world would have only been what I saw on a southern dirt road. Now I also understand, from watching TV, that I am more of a visual learner.

Watching *Sesame Street* and Counting with Count Dracula enhanced the other lessons provided to me by my family. Because of the aspects of patience, counting with the Muppets was a lot more fun than trying to learn to count with my older brothers.

When I did make it to kindergarten, it was a half day. And I attended the afternoon session. My mom would drop me off, and I would ride the bus home every day with kids as old as high school seniors.

That seems strange now; a five-year-old kid had no business being on the same bus with seniors. Plus, dealing with racism was rough only five years after the feds had to force the south to integrate. However, I was fortunate enough to have older siblings and a black bus driver, Mr. J.T. Hunter, to look out for me.

Mr. Hunter was also the barber who cut our family's hair. His precision and skill as a barber inspired my interest in the profession early in my life. As a World War II veteran, he was attentive to details on our bus. When we got too rowdy, we could always look up and see him looking right at us in his rearview mirror. That stare was his way of telling us to keep it down.

One day a white senior called Mr. Hunter a nigger. He let the young man slide by saying, "All right now son, you need to go on back there and sit down."

The redneck sat right behind me and made a subtle reference to my hair looking like pubic hair. But I wasn't worried because I saw that Mr. J.T. had his eyes right on him! He again told the boy, "All right now son, keep it down," as he drove our bus down a narrow dirt road.

While at the same time, out of the corner of my eye, I saw one of my older brothers' friends, Pope, ball up his fist tightly, while keeping his middle knuckle sticking out, as if it were an additional weapon extending his fist. We often did that to imitate a black wrestler named Thunderbolt Patterson.

When the redneck made another general statement using the *n*-word again, Pope jumped up and straddled him. He pushed the boy's head back over the bus seat with one hand and, with machine-gun rapid-fire consistency, Pope continuously kept striking the redneck repeatedly with his Thunderbolt Patterson fist!

Usually, Mr. Hunter would have intervened way before a fight became that outwardly engaged. However, on that day, he was a tiny bit delayed in seeing what was happening right behind him. Pope beat that poor boy up until he was completely exhausted.

No one broke the fight up. Thunderbolt Pope beat the young man up so long that even his protruding knuckle had flattened out! When it was finally time for the redneck to get off the bus, Mr. Hunter asked while looking directly in his rearview mirror, "Hey son! Are you all right back there?"

Another student had to help the guy up. He was still dazed as he stumbled off the bus. The guy wobbled as he walked toward his home, which had a Confederate flag hanging off the porch. The punch-drunk senior staggered toward his house in a manner that made me think he created the Cha-Cha Slide way back in the 1970s.

The next day, the redneck had a totally different attitude on the bus. Mr. Hunter asked him if he was okay as he got on. The guy seemed to be an overnight convert, because he addressed Mr. Hunter with the respect our elders deserve, replying, "Yes sir." As we rode the bus together, I noticed that the senior's head looked as swollen as Martin Lawrence's on the episode in which he had a boxing match with Thomas "The Hitman" Hearns.

The mean things older kids said hurt but they never bothered me in the long term. The power words from my mother had already filled the void deep within me: "You're no better than anyone else, but you're certainly not any less than anyone else either. Don't you dare ever let nobody treat you like you are any less." Her power mantra sustains me to this day.

Our parents attended all-black schools in the South. The system was separate but not even close to being equal. When the white kids would get new books, they would intentionally tear out some of the pages from their old books before they passed them down to black children. Another hindrance for black schools was heat in the winters. Black schools relied on potbellied stoves for heat, and almost no school had buses for their students.

On top of that, my uncles said that they had to walk for miles to get to school, only to be passed by new school buses transporting the white children to school. To add further insult to injury, my uncles said that when the buses passed them, white kids would yell and throw things at them walking, from the luxury of their privileged comfort as they rode by.

Our mom also shared with me about the tough and trying times when white kids from Holsenbeck School would see them walking home and rush out of the safety of their school, just to become bad barriers in blockage to carelessly obstruct the black children's only narrow path home.

It was then, with unwavering pride my mother's fearless little sister Lois would bore her way right through the evil mob of young terrorists-in-training, without flinching. It was the boldness of little Lois that gave all the other black children the courage to follow in her path right on through the cruel "cute" mob of future right-wing extremist, in basic training.

These accounts are very detailed. And the abuse our ancestors survived while growing up in the segregated South provides our society incites of actual historical data. Treasure droves of information like this was the intentionally torn out pages of the books our parents were handed down from white students.

That is why it is of upmost importance that we bridge the gap by passing down these crucial stories like elders in an African village. Because when we do share our ancestors' testimonies, we are properly placing those purposely missing pages back.

What our people endured was critical. It was all about race. Yet it wasn't just a "theory". The critical circumstances black folks endure was because of race. It's hard to fix a problem when you refuse to face it. America the beautiful cannot truly see her beauty until she faces herself.

We must see ourselves in the mirror. And then maybe if we rebranded critical race theory and just called it the truth, we might be able to get some folks to listen before they lose their minds complaining about CRT. I've always said we wouldn't need African American history month if we taught actual American history all year.

Of course, I do question some of the specific details I've heard at the barbershop. An old man once told me he had to walk ten miles, to and from school, uphill both ways in a severe snowstorm down south. With all due respect, I question the landscape or the way the weather treated our ancestors; however, I will never doubt the cruel way in which people treated us back then.

It was worse than most can recall. Chris Rock said, "My mother had to get her teeth taken out at the vet [an animal doctor]. No civil rights movie shows you that!"

You will never convince me to think that the white children who were throwing rocks and blocking the roads were born with those evil qualities; someone taught them that. In the US, you can send a child to school only hoping they will become a future farmer but after twelve years they could graduate with honors into joining the Future Right-Wing Extremist of America.

Those poor, misguided souls have to have the support of their churches and schools to sustain that level of animus towards people of color. Replicated hateful behaviors need systems to survive. These tentacles need many sources to become nourished, taught, and reproduced over time.

Since we have a history of duplicating the same misguided products over time, we must face the fact that America has many factories hidden all around us. Meanwhile, these hate plants are hidden amongst us in plain sight. We are not simply dealing with just a few bad apples; these regenerated apples come in bad bunches and hang like strange fruit from southern trees.

Our fruits are cultivated by corrupt croppers whose hearts are so drenched with detestation that they have contaminated our soil. A byproduct of our contaminated soil is what we call our Constitution.

The US Constitution says that a black person is three-fifths of a human being; on top of that, the three-fifths clause granted southerners more representation in Congress to vote against the rights of those who were considered fractions of a person.

Then those representatives who were given the power to vote on the behalf of us, "as fractions of human beings", abused their misguided authority to create slave patrols. Or, as we say now, in our present time, the police.

Those patrols were and are still used, in a way, to help slave owners maintain control of "their property". Consider this, the population of the United States is 5 percent of the world's population, but we have 25 percent of the world's incarcerated people.

There should be no doubt that these tentacles of the state are disproportionately targeted at black and brown boys. As we dig further, we need not look too far to see how these tentacles continue attaching themselves to our children.

The Literacy Project Foundation found that three out of five people in US prisons can't read, three out of four on welfare can't read, and 85 percent of juvenile offenders have trouble reading. Reimagining the rural South doesn't require us to reinvent it. However, in reimagining any kind of a future for our children we must reinvest into reading programs, for everyone.

It is our inaction on this literacy crisis that is the great crime of our time! Our society has been so laser-focused on accommodating the problem that we haven't invested a fraction of that fuel in finding less costly and far more compassionate solutions.

Looking at the numbers, it is clear that literacy rates correlate inversely with incarceration rates. If we look closer into our mirror, it's easy to see that providing people with books is more heartwarming than cycling citizens through prison cells. Our empathetic solutions require us to stop giving up on a great portion of our population and counter balance our efforts towards literacy projects.

I love literacy programs, such as Leap for Literacy, which promotes literacy in underserved communities. It was founded by Statham's very own Stan Tucker. Stan and his book *Stan and the Man* made it from the one-red-light town of Statham, Georgia, all the way to the bright lights of *The Ellen DeGeneres Show*.

It humbles me to be in the grass on this side of the tracks of that young man's life's journey. Stan's story influenced me to write my own. To hear Stan's story of how his small-town barber had a positive influence on his life is absolutely humbling. In fact, Stan's story was an inspiration reciprocated back to me for this book. Inspiration is contagious as a guide to liberating the rural South.

Barbering is a big deal in our communities. Research has showed me how I too could have a great influence on those I serve. Realizing that has given my purpose a greater responsibility to work with others invested in helping the next generation of readers. This barber's goal is for one person to say that my book is the first entire book that they've ever read! Understanding that, reading reveals other paths to liberation.

Barbers are some children's first direct encounters with black businessmen. By simply being a positive visual representation, you might inspire the next Alonzo Herndon. Alonzo was a barber born in our neighboring Walton County, Georgia, on June 26, 1858. He became a barber, and he founded the Atlanta Family Life Insurance Company.

Herndon also became one of the first African American millionaires. His success had a major influence on those in his community. Positivity has rippling effects in this world of good vibrations. Sending out good vibes should be your motivation to get up every day. My barber, Mr. J.T. Hunter, had an enormous influence on my life. The source of inspiration for many people has come from behind a compassionate barber's chair.

It is especially important in these rural spaces to be great examples for our impressionable young minds. For there are many forces trying to kill young black boys' spirits in small-town America. You could be the one light to counterbalance all of the negative noise our boys might encounter today.

Some of the southern noise reaches our children's ears through athletics. When I was about nine, I played football for the Statham Warriors. Our colors were green and gold. Mr. McKendrick was our coach.

At our first practice, he gathered our team and said, "All right guys, we want to make things fun for everyone! I'll go around and let you all introduce yourselves and tell me which position you'd like to try out for. Remember, you might not win the position you want, but I promise you that everyone will get a fair chance."

This was around 1980, so everybody wanted to be O.J. Simpson; almost everyone said he wanted to play running back. Even the slowest kid on our team dreamed he was fast like the Juice running through the airport in those Hertz commercials.

When the coach asked me, which position I wanted to play, I chose to be different. "I want to be the quarterback," I said. The entire football field went quieter than a mouse pissing on cotton.

Coach said, "Quarterback?" It was as if I had said something wrong. This was before Randall Cunningham played quarterback for the Philadelphia Eagles and before the record-breaking Doug Williams won a Super Bowl as quarterback with the Washington football team. The quarterback position for black men at that time was taboo.

When I listen to sports analysts today, it still sounds as if the quarterback position is viewed through a different lens when the QB is a person of color. For instance, Russell Wilson, the Super Bowl–winning quarterback for the Seahawks, is often applauded by commentators for his agility and mobility; while there is often an unconscious reluctance to compliment the man on his IQ.

When it is clear that Wilson is a man of supreme wisdom and not just for his brilliance in reading defenses and baiting them with the surgical precision of his spectacular throws. Good Lord, the man is obviously a genius for marrying Ciara! Give the brother his due credit.

Nevertheless, in those days, me verbalizing my desire to play quarterback was a no-no. Some coaches didn't appreciate aspirational black kids back then, and some still don't like inspired black kids now. Those insecure coaches fear we might one day grow up to understand that, he who has no imagination has no wings.

Those southerners who are accustomed to dealing with shrinking negroes know that it is harder to convince a grown person to reduce their expectations when they have been taught they can fly as a kid. Therefore, because my coach felt the need to reduce my aspirations, I went from wanting to be the quarterback to hiking the ball to the quarterback at center.

Although the process deflated my spirits, I remained committed to the team. In the view of the fact that I was taught if you work hard in life, life will always give you a chance. And as it turned out somehow, life actually did.

The starting quarterback—the coach's son—was really uncoordinated. His throwing motion was so erratic that one time, the coach told him to try throwing the ball with his other hand to see if that would work better.

The season started, and it only took two games for us to become the joke of our town. On one play, our quarterback was supposed to hand the ball off to the right, but his afflicted feet got so tangled up that he pitched the ball left to an opposing player, who caught it and ran for a touchdown the other way.

The parents' quiet murmurs turned into angry screams. Our coach was especially humiliated since the quarterback was his son. After that play, the coach abruptly said to me, "Barnard you're in!"

I put my helmet on. "Coach, what plays are we running?"

Coach just shrugged. "I'm sure you'll figure something out."

The coach didn't send me out there with the first-team or even the second-team offense; he sent me out with no plays and the guys who hadn't played at all. And to top that off, Coach put us on the field with the slowest player in the world as our tailback. This is no exaggeration, we are still waiting on the guy's forty-yard dash time, because it is a for-ever.

As we trotted onto the field, before we could even get into the huddle, the slowest player started expressing how much he wanted to run like O.J. I knew I could not blow this chance by calling the play for Slow Jay; our team was already the laughingstock of the league because of our other QB. Therefore, I had to take command of the huddle over Slow Jay's pleas, so I barked out, "Fullback dive right! Break!"

Our fullback was a very small fragile kid named Robbie. After I handed Robbie the ball, he squirted through the line so quickly that the defense didn't see him until it was too late. Robbie got us all the way to the opposing team's two-yard line.

When we got back to the huddle, everybody was happy, except our slowest tailback in the nation. "Come on Barnard! Please let me run the ball!" he begged. "I may never get a chance in my life to ever score a touchdown."

A flood of water centered his eyes and I heard the humanity and desperation in his voice. So, I called the play for Slow Jay to run left off tackle. "Break!"

Slow Jay was so excited before the snap that I thought he would give our play call away. Thus, I rushed behind center and snapped the ball quickly. As I handed the football to Slow Jay, he was so slow he caused the entire game to go into slow motion. The hole waiting on him off left tackle was so wide open it looked like the parted Red Sea. Patiently, the world waited for Slow Jay to hit the gap.

Have you ever seen the Burt Reynolds movie *The Longest Yard*? This was more like the longest a thousand miles. I could have walked to the concession stand, used the restroom twice, and made it back to the field before Slow Jay finally stumbled and fell face-first into the end zone.

Touchdown! We all were happy to see Slow Jay get his first and only score. However, when we got back to the sidelines, we could see that our coach didn't appreciate his own team's success. Our coach's plan had been to undermine his own team of kids by not providing us with any plays.

Also, Coach thought he had doomed us by putting the slowest kid on the planet in a position in which speed is a main requirement. Yet God can take what man meant for evil and use it for good! I never got a chance to play quarterback again, but I'll always feel good about calling the play for Slow Jay to score a touchdown.

Reflecting back now I realize how critical visual representation is in inspiring us to see ourselves in a myriad of positions. In the 1970s, there were not many brave black men portrayed on TV. Because of that, I was stuck idolizing white daredevils. Before the movie *Jackass*, there was Evel Knievel. And I really wanted to be like him.

Donnie, my older cousin, would set up ramps for me and my go-kart to jump over dangerous things. Once, he used a thin sheet of plywood as a ramp for me to jump over the trailer my dad pulled his tractor on. I was full speed on my way up the ramp, about to jump the trailer, when the plywood broke in half, and my body jackknifed right into the metal trailer.

Semiconscious, I sat there in a dust cloud so thick that anyone who saw it would have thought Jesus was coming back right then. Donnie ran over to my flailed body and said, "Man! You almost made it. Now, give me the Evel Knievel thumbs-up!"

I tried to do everything Donnie asked me to, but on that day I couldn't, because it felt like the metal trailer had ripped my entire arm off. I still have a scar on my arm as a reminder to never attempt to jump the Grand Canyon.

The subtleties of racism are magnified by the conditions of isolation in the Deep South. Sometimes we accept our small-town conditions created by small minded people as if we are not connected to the rest of the world.

Think about how the three murderers of Ahmaud Arbery would have never gotten arrested much less convicted in Brunswick, Georgia without outside divine intervention. It wasn't until the activist took the horrors of small-town Americans to the rest of the world that we finally got some justice for Ahmaud's mother, Wanda Cooper-Jones.

When I was growing up, we lived on one side of the train tracks, with few places to cross. If a train stalled, it could be a long wait to get to the other side. On the other side of the tracks, one could at least have access to highways to get out of town.

Timing was a must, though. There were many times when we would be riding along and a train would come and stop us in our tracks. When that happened, time stood still; and there was nothing we could do but sit there, sometimes, for hours in a hot car.

Once, my sister, Carol, was learning to drive my brother James's new five-speed Nissan Maxima. They got to the train tracks, and the car stalled out. Moments later, a train was coming, and the stick-shift car stalled out again and would not restart.

Thankfully, Carol and James got out of the car before the train took the Maxima for a joy ride down the tracks. Cars are replaceable, but people are not. That's just one of the memories I have on the importance of getting on over the tracks.

Another memory I have is of my father asking me something as we prepared to drive over the railroad crossing. I wanted to give my father what I thought was the right answer instead of what was just true. But it's hard to figure out what to say when you are not being totally honest.

Before Dad bothered to look up the tracks to see if a train was coming, he looked at me and said, "Boy don't you lie to me!" His words resonated with me in a way that affects me until this day.

That moment was a rite of passage for me; it taught me that a man should say what he means and mean what he says. I believe my father understood that my coming of age needed to come a bit sooner. I was nowhere near my teens when that conversation happened. But from that moment on, I tried to speak honestly.

That doesn't mean I have never spoken an untruth since that conversation with my father. It means from that instance forward, I've been uncomfortable with being dishonest with my family, my community, and, most importantly, myself. The platform was established for the importance of living in authenticity.

Mr. Leon Kincy, a sharply dressed black man who was my counselor at Athens Technical College, confirmed the seed my father had planted in me without him knowing it. His recorded message on his answering machine was "This is Leon Kincy. Tell the truth, and you will not have to remember a story. Please leave a message?"

Although today sincerity can get you into trouble, and telling lies can make you the president. Donald Trump's lies paved his way to the presidency of the United States of America. And my father's wisdom would have never been able to fathom that. How could a society who really thinks that truth and justice are the American way, end up with a president like Trump?

In spite of that, my father's words still encourage me to embrace genuineness. The truth is, that speaking facts can make you feel like it is what causes the trouble but it is not.

The righteous John Lewis called it getting into good trouble. As civil rights activists, we understand that the truth will set you free. In contrast to knowing that, what do you think lying will do? Lying keeps us in bondage. Candor is essential to a black man's guide to liberating the rural South.

In barbering people with different perspectives and personalities are coming into our spaces every single day. And if we change the gospel just to agree with everyone who walks through our doors, by the end of the day, how we really feel and who we really are can be lost.

We can lose a car. We can lose a father. But we cannot afford to lose ourselves. When Muhammad Ali lost his fight against Leon Spinks, he said, "In life, you're going to lose something." Ali's example proves you can overcome losses and still be the greatest ever! All is never lost as long as you never lose yourself.

Researching who we truly are helps us to root ourselves in a divine righteousness. Envisioning ourselves based on what we find when we discover our history before the transatlantic slave trade enables us to connect with the chosen people we are to be today.

Knowing the seeds from which we came from, gives us the confidence we need as a race of people to face these rural pockets of oppression. For it is this liberating of our minds that will spark the genesis of our revelation!

Postulate 3

THE HARVEST IS PLENTY—
THE COMPLAINERS NEED TO BE FEW

HOW DID RACE make America so dysfunctional? Why do white folks hate us so much? What did we ever do to them? Baffled adults come into the barbershop all the time asking plenty of those types of questions. Even little children are observant enough to see that so much is still wrong.

When my youngest daughter was eight, she asked, "Daddy, why is that police officer just sitting on George Floyd's neck? Can't he see that the man can't breathe?" As fathers we try to encourage our children to ask the right questions. As parents we search our souls to provide the most accurate answers to those pressing questions.

However, as a dad, I realized that my daughter's simple question was way too complicated for any decent human being to have an answer for. Good people don't understand why an officer would mash the life out of a man like a bug.

Children are not born with this level of disdain for other human beings. It is horrible what blacks, Native Americans, Latinos, Asians, Jews, and the LGBTQ communities have endured for centuries. It takes a system to program us to be this insensitive to the levels of injustices we still see until this very day.

Why must it take protest to get an arrest, in hopes of a lengthy trial, just to convince mature adults of what my eight-year-old daughter knew was wrong instantly? What decent human being needs to be convinced that it is not right for a police officer to sit on a man's neck until he dies? It takes centuries of being desensitized to violence and the inhumane treatment of an entire culture for us to have to wonder if that type of murderous behavior is acceptable or not.

The psychological programming for these systems that desensitizes our society of our common humanity has to start in some suburban American homes. The elders always cite the African proverb that it takes a village to raise a child. However, it hinders the village if we are raising home-grown terrorists in our huts! We must help the village by programming our children with love and tolerance for others in our huts.

For instance, our cement construction company was working in a suburban subdivision pouring cement driveways, walkways, and car porches in Auburn, Georgia, around 1990. Mack, a coworker, was driving the tractor from one job site to the next.

Out of nowhere, two white kids who couldn't have been older than six or seven came blasting out to the street to throw rocks at us. We didn't see the incident as racial at first, until the kids approached us after the tractor stopped. The two little boys came up to us and politely asked, "Niggers?"

Mack and I looked at each other.

The two white kids harmoniously chimed in again. "Niggers. Niggers?"

Mack finally looked at the two white children as if to acknowledge hearing their racial slurs. The boys then looked Mack right in his face and said, "Nigger!"

Mack took a deep breath and asked, "What do you want?"

The kids, satisfied that one of us had responded to the word *nigger*, simply looked at Mack, and said, "We just wanted to say hi."

After the strange encounter, we went right back to work doing our job.

Puzzled, I asked Mack, "Why did you respond so kindly to us being called niggers?"

Mack replied, "Because those children don't know no better. Those kids are being taught that ignorance from inside of their house. If you follow a stupid kid home, chances are that a stupid parent will answer the door. Now, if those kids' daddy comes out here and calls me a nigger, I'm going to kick his ass to teach those kids a good lesson!"

Although Mack's way is one way to learn today, however the best good lessons start from within the hut. That doesn't mean the village should give up on teaching just because some don't get taught at home. When youth are not taught at home, it is not their fault.

The village still has a responsibility, because as another African proverb says, "A child who is not embraced by the village will burn it down to feel its warmth." We still need to make sure our youth feel loved by their communities.

Nonetheless, negligence in the hut makes it much harder for the village to connect our youth with the guidance they need and the warmth of love they yearn for.

In my family's hut, I was taught not to look down on anyone and to put no man before God. Yet outside our home, components of inferiority were infused into us when we tried to assimilate into a white society.

Over time, the effects of this way of life can reduce our self-esteems. The subtle microaggressions that thrive throughout our society cause a many of us to fold by unconsciously self-subordinating ourselves into roles of second-class citizenship. Many of us do this without even realizing that we are minimizing ourselves. We are subliminally hypnotized into a psychological state of devaluing our own existence just to survive and get by.

In addition, we often recite catchphrases that sound good, such as, "Education is the great equalizer." Well if education is the great equalizer, then why are black women getting advanced degrees at the highest rate in America (according to the National Center for Educational Statistics), but they are only earning sixty-three cents to every white man's dollar? That math doesn't add up to equality. Education does help, but it cannot accurately claim to be the great equalizer. Men lie, and women lie, but numbers don't lie.

Today in public schools all across America, we know that black and brown students are less likely to be recommended for gifted programs but they are more likely to be suspended. One reason for these disparities traces back to implicit biases.

The National Center for Education Statistics reports that nearly 80 percent of the teachers in the United States are white. My alma mater, Winder Barrow High School, reported that its total minority student enrollment was 43 percent. Even in the Deep South, teachers look way different from the student bodies they serve.

Many black students are forced to survive in a sea plagued with low expectations for them. There is no scientific data that one can present to prove that black and brown people are intellectually inferior to white people.

There is also no proof that black children are genetically predisposed to underachievement. So why do these narratives exist? If I am really being honest, as my father taught me to be, I would have an easier time trying to prove that the opposite is true. Untapped reserves of black excellence are everywhere! The harvest is plenty, but simply complaining about the harvest won't do.

For instance, Benjamin Banneker was a descendant of the Dogon tribe. The Dogon people from West Africa are known for being gifted in the science of astronomy. The founding fathers used Benjamin Banneker's brilliance to create the almanac and clocks to help them keep accurate time.

Thomas Jefferson, one of those founders, needs a documentary made about him, like *Surviving R. Kelly*. But it was Benjamin Banneker's gifts that were used to help survey the boundaries of our nation's capital.

Knowing these historical facts about the intellectual genius of blacks who have contributed greatly to this great nation allows us to grow in our pride and esteem. As my mother said, "You aren't better than anybody else, but you're definitely not any less than nobody else either."

Yet and still today, the data shows that black students are being recommended for gifted programs and Advanced Placement courses at a lower rate than white students.

Using national data from the Early Childhood Longitudinal Study, Sean Nicholson-Crotty, PhD, and his colleagues at Indiana University found that black students were 54 percent less likely than white students to be recommended for gifted programs. While at the same time, black students were three times more likely to be referred to these programs if their teacher was black rather than white.

So, let's get this straight: The harvest is plenty if you are suspending our children, but if you are recommending our kids for AP courses, we are supposed to believe that the harvest is few?

I'm sure you have heard about black students being overlooked and mistreated by our school systems. We have witnessed many times where a black student had earned their high school's valedictorian honor when suddenly the school's rules change and the deserving black student is asked to share that honor with a white student of privilege. We know our children are very smart. Somehow, our children's brilliance goes less detected in our schools.

Two of my godsons were reading before they started school. Their mother dedicated herself to reading to them before they came out of her womb. I knew these two kids were extremely intelligent by the way they conversed with me about adult issues or whatever the topic was in the barbershop. My godsons were well read and mathematical geniuses by the time they started school here in Barrow County.

Their persistent mother had them tested, and our school system said neither had made high enough scores to be in the gifted program. She reluctantly accepted the Barrow County school system's findings.

However, by chance of a mother's persistence, my godsons moved to our neighboring Clarke County, whose school system has a black superintendent as well as far more diversity in leadership positions. Within the first week there, the teachers recognized how smart my godsons were, and they immediately put both of them in the gifted program, based off of the same test scores that Barrow County took!

A few years later, after my godsons moved back, the Barrow County school system tried to put them back in regular classes, although both boys were doing extremely well in the gifted program in Athens! Thankfully, their mother didn't let that happen; both finished school with honors and went off to college. Thank God for mothers who understand we must fight for our black boys!

What changed? Did those two boys get smarter just by moving to a more diverse district? There is no geographical explanation to explain how moving two black boys ten miles away from their homes made them smarter.

Educational bias and lack of communication with parents are two of the reasons black students are below the national average in being placed in Advanced Placement courses in our schools. My family experienced this truth firsthand too. Thankfully, the only black teacher in our daughter's school at the time was the advocate who recognized that our daughter belonged in AP classes.

Around 2011, I was working with the local NAACP, and I served on the school committee. Part of our research was finding out how many black and brown teachers we had in our school system. The numbers reported back to us would've had us in disbelief if we hadn't already been paying attention. The moment you walk into either of our now 16 schools, it is easy to see that there are very few of us teaching but a whole lot of us sweeping!

At that time, our district had fourteen schools with 1,022 educators, but only 29 (2.8 percent) of them were black or Hispanic. We set up a meeting with our superintendent realizing that our student population was becoming more racially balanced, in terms of diversity, and we thought that our teachers should better reflect the students they served as well.

Our superintendent looked me dead in the face and said, "Barnard, we can't lower our standards just to hire black teachers."

We were offended on many levels because we had not submitted one résumé to her at that time. What made the superintendent think she needed to lower her standards to hire black and brown people?

Remember, black women are the most educated demographic of people in the United States. Therefore, how does anyone instinctively believe that black and brown people must be less qualified?

In addition, I didn't understand what standards the superintendent was referring to, for at that time, our local Winder Barrow High School was on Georgia's list of Focus Schools. WBHS, under Principal Al Darby, stayed on the low-achievement list due to our school's low graduation rate; the school is also plagued by a perpetual achievement gap. I am saying all of this so that you will understand, that the standards our superintendent was referencing were already pretty darn low!

When I was on our school's governance team, I learned about the achievement gap. Let's say 69 percent of white students passed a standardized test, and only 45 percent of Latino and African American students passed the same standardized test. That's a big achievement gap, right? In the words of Rodney Dangerfield, "We can't get no respect!" And we shouldn't expect any respect as long as we are producing dire numbers like that in our educational system.

There were many times during those meetings when I was the lone black man in the room with educators who would comfortably claim, "We're getting better as a school system. Our scores for black children came up two percent!"

I would sit there in amazement. Because I didn't think that 45 percent of any group of children passing a standardized test was a cause for a celebration. Frankly, I don't think that 69 percent of white students passing a test is a good enough reason to have a parade with the World Series winning Atlanta Braves either.

When I expressed my dissatisfaction for the room's comfortable acceptance of failing numbers, I, the lone black man, became the cause of the problem to them. Those educators could not see that our failing grades should've been our real focus to fix.

Instead, those blurry lensed leaders chose to blame the lone black man for pointing out the facts. I will proudly take the blame for not shrinking my expectations for the excellence I see in our children. Scores of 43, 45, and 69 are not passing grades. Our children deserve our best; and if they fail, that means we have failed them.

There is no proof of a genetic predisposition to explain why Latinos would underperform scholastically. Most of the Latino children I've worked with at our Boys and Girls Club already speak two languages, and some are working on a third or fourth.

Why is there an achievement gap anyway? I have found a consistent correlation: where there are gaps, there is usually a lack of hired diverse employees. In contrast, the best-performing schools in our nation typically show the opposite.

For instance, the Preuss School in California reports that 99.6 percent of its students are economically disadvantaged, but it and many other high schools in California rank highly in student achievement. Correlating with those schools' success, is the diversity represented in those schools' leadership and staff.

The harvest is plenty. We have to be resourceful enough to engage one another, utilizing the gospel of inclusion. Every single person adds significance and value to the harvest. What we must do is to open the gates for everyone's gifts. That is the best way to properly prepare the next generation of diverse leaders.

As Joe Madison, the Black Eagle, says, "We are culturally conditioned to believe that White is superior and Black is inferior. And the manifestation of that cultural conditioning is that Black people are undervalued, underestimated, and marginalized."

We accept negative perceptions and circulate those false beliefs in our own communities. I could write another book on cultural conditioning and how we undervalue ourselves.

I am the sole proprietor of Barnard's Hair Salon. And I cannot count the number of people who have asked me, "Do you ever get tired of just cutting hair?" My answer is no, I never undervalue my ability to create art on demand to make a living, and no, I don't underestimate the value of providing a needed service to our community. The question itself is condescending.

Usually, those who ask me that question get up from my chair and run to work for somebody else. Those who work for others should never marginalize the value of what entrepreneurs do for a living.

The way a man thinks, so is he. I was the chess coach for Mauri, a confident black child. Chess and Community Conference, a nonprofit founded by Life the Griot, had an annual regional chess tournament in Athens, Georgia, on the University of Georgia's college campus.

In the first round of the tournament, Mauri was paired against an Asian American kid. I noticed that Mauri's swag dissipated before he even made his first move, and he lost terribly. I pulled him to the side and asked, "What happened to your confidence son? You gave that game away."

"Coach, you know I can't beat no Asian kid," he answered.

It took all of me not to cuss! I responded, "You listen here Mauri. Do you know that there are pyramids still standing that your ancestors-built thousands of years ago? Son, do you understand that archaeologists and architects today are still trying to figure out how your ancestors built them?

Those black geniuses looked just like you. Going forward Mauri, you wear that knowledge as your source of pride. We are not intellectually inferior to anyone, and don't you ever sit down across the table from anyone else unless you totally believe that!"

Mauri looked me in the eye with his swag completely back. He played against children from every ethnicity and didn't lose another game for the rest of the tournament.

Imagine if we had more diversity in our schools to connect those dots, for our children. The information has been there waiting to reach us for years. Our ability to connect the harvest to who we are is key to the awakening!

This achievement gap is evidence that we are missing the pieces to bridge the gap across all cultures. Every school system must learn to connect the dots for children of color too. I recall speaking at one of our school board meetings on the issue of our low achievement scores and how the scores correlated with our need for more diversity hires.

At the end, I said, "The Georgia Academy for the Blind is a school with all ethnicities represented, and there is not an achievement gap in sight. If the Georgia School for the Blind can figure this out, surely, we can too, especially since we're all sitting here looking right at each other."

Shannon Sharpe said, "The person who cannot see is really not the blindest. The person who chooses not to see is."

The room was silent in solidarity, but God heard me, and most of the time, that is enough. We submitted a list of qualified black and brown teachers to our school system, but not one was hired that year. We then went to our Equal Employment Opportunity Commission in Atlanta and filed a formal complaint against the Barrow County school system for racial discrimination. We reported the numbers I mentioned earlier: out of 1,022 teachers, only about 2 percent were black or Latino.

The EEOC agent said those numbers alone were a red flag, and they investigated the matter; we ended up getting a new superintendent. However, even with the current superintendent, the culture is still the same. In the one NAACP meeting our superintendent and our then district one school board representative Debi Krause attended,—not coincidentally near election time—, they were both excited that our school district's diversity had inched up 3 percent.

Also, not coincidentally, school board representative Debi Krause's son-in-law was hired as vice principal of a school in her district.

Nepotism is the cradle for exclusion. I am black, and my wife is black, and if we only seek out to hire our children, guess what our work space is going to look like? The chances are that the work space is going to be all black. In a large place, such as a school system, nepotism allows work spaces to discriminate against people of color.

We still have a lot of work to do in challenging the structures of those environments. Our struggle continues in the rural South, but be ye not discouraged. Know that the harvest is plenty!

In conjunction, according to the US Department of Education, Office for Civil Rights, black students are 3.8 times more likely to get suspended than white students are.

What makes that statistic even more disturbing is the fact that black students are 2.3 times more likely to be referred to law enforcement or school resource officers. This creates the gateway that channels our children as fuel for the school-to-prison pipeline.

Often, when we discuss that school-to-prison pipeline, we follow the pipeline directly to the prison. But those tracks leave prison and pass right back through the town of Poverty. Then those tracks double-back to the town called Prison again.

According to the NAACP's Fair Chance Hiring Fact Sheet, white men with criminal records are more likely to be interviewed for jobs than black men with no criminal records. Poverty results from lack of sustainable employment. The dominos all fall into place, causing crime to increase in areas where people are poor.

It is strange that we are programmed to associate criminality with blackness rather than poverty. For instance, if we had ten black cats and ten white cats and starved them all for a couple of days, guess which color of cats would be scavenging through your open garbage can tonight?

It would not be the blackest or the whitest cats; it would simply be the hungriest cats trying to survive. My point is that criminality has almost everything to do with poverty and absolutely nothing to do with pigmentation.

One would think the church would be the institution to lead our society in sorting out these disparities. However, what we find is that a major obstruction from us mending these fences is our churches. In 1963, Dr. Martin Luther King Jr. said, "It is appalling that the most segregated hour of Christian America is eleven o'clock on Sunday morning." It is more appalling that King's statement is still true nearly sixty years later.

On every corner of every community across this nation are churches named First Baptist, First Methodist, First United—First this and First that. However, when it comes to the concerns affecting issues across the color lines in those same communities, those same churches become the Last Baptist, Last Methodist because they are the last to unite and the last to act. Even the more influential churches, such as Joel Osteen and 12Stone, seem silent when it comes to racial reconciliation.

Let's explore how some of the most blatant and sinister theories find platforms in our churches. Our local Bethlehem First Baptist Church's former pastor, Jody Hice, was catapulted into the national spotlight when he and thirty-three other pastors across America chose to focus on political issues from their pulpits in 2007 and 2008.

Their religious cult called it Pulpit Freedom Sunday. Can you guess what the churches' driving, motivating force was that took the focus away from saving souls? Was Pulpit Freedom every Sunday in America since 1789?

Pulpit Freedom Sunday only started when America chose to elect its first African American president. The timeline of silence until First Baptist Church's first uproar leaves no other reasoning for their messages of intolerance and hate. To make it plain, First Baptist chose to protest our first African American president—period—and that isn't Christlike.

Sadly, leaders, such as Jody Hice and Donald Trump, stoke the flames of racial fears for political gain. Hice used this sinister platform from his pulpit to become the US representative for Georgia's tenth congressional district.

In 2016, Trump used the same southern strategy to become the president. The Trump movement was built on the sinister notion that President Obama was somehow an illegitimate citizen. This Trump birther movement became so extreme in the South that the Don duped people into believing that even a baby born to a white woman from the heartland of Kansas wasn't American enough for them.

Out of fear, people in the South bought into the lies hook, line, and sinker. Trump lost the popular vote but did carry the demographic of voters he was seeking in the South: uneducated rural white voters. White southerners came out in masse to support the man, regardless of what he said.

According to CNN exit polls, 71 percent of white men who were not college graduates voted for Donald Trump, as did 61 percent of the white women who were not college graduates.

This, of course, does not mean that everyone who voted for Trump was white, rural, and uneducated. It does mean, however, that if you voted for Trump, your vote was cast with the white, rural, and uneducated voters. That is just a truth we must consider if we hope to do better.

The other part of the equation is that 80 percent of the born-again or evangelical white Christians voted for Trump, according to the same CNN poll. The statistics prove that religious dogma was an effective tool in manipulating the largest group of voters in America.

Again, that doesn't necessarily mean that 80 percent of the white evangelicals who voted for Trump were white, rural, and uneducated. I would never say that. However, it does mean that 80 percent of those Christians voted for a man who paid a porn star $130,000 to keep quiet

It also means that 80 percent of those so-called evangelicals voted for a man shown in videos cuddling it up with, child sex predator, Jerry Epstein. In addition, it does mean that 80 percent of the white so-called Christians gave their full support to a man caught on tape saying it was okay to grab women by their private parts, without their consent, while he was married to his third wife. I'm only saying that evangelicals must have some rock star Christian values, right?

Did those Christians consider that the values Trump displayed are in total contrast to the moral values that they claim to have? The banner boy for the religious right was somehow able to misuse Christianity as the cross to carry Donald J. Trump over the goal post in becoming our nations 45th president. Hoisting their hero over their shoulders was the white, rural and uneducated voters. These poor misguided souls were manipulated by religious dogma and stoked by their racial fears.

Customers often come into the barbershop with culturally self-degrading, programmed preconceived ideas. To counter those false perceptions, our dialogue gets heated in a way that only conversations in our barbershops and beauty salons can. What I've observed is that there is this narrative in our own community to blame blacks first for everything. I'm all for taking personal responsibility, but based on the facts I just cited, you can't logically blame black voters for Trump.

In the barbershop, I would hear people say that black voters did not turn out for Hillary Clinton the same way they did for President Obama. That is true. However, given all the voter-suppression laws used to discourage us in America, we should not be expected to turn out at 100 percent for every election.

That is the aspirational goal; however, always putting the burden of responsibility on the backs of black people to save our nation is not fair. Other groups need to step up as well. Growing up, we were told we needed to be three times better to get half a chance. That is an undue heavy weight of excessive pressure to be unfairly placed on an entire group of pigmented people's backs. Plus, this nation owes black people way more than just a half-a-chance.

If all things are equal, then we can and should properly place the blame for Donald Trump's catastrophic presidency exactly where it belongs. In the case of our past president Trump, the real blame should be with white women. Fifty-two percent of white women voted for Trump rather than someone who could've been the first female president.

Hillary Clinton was probably the most experienced political candidate our nation has ever seen, male or female. What other president has ever been able to say, on their resume, that I also served as first lady to the president for 8 years?

Yet the majority of white women voted for a misogynist. Therefore, some of the blame should be placed squarely at Cinderella's feet. In closing arguments, the great attorney Johnnie Cochran might have said, "If Cinderella's slippers fit, some of the blame she must get."

Understand that when black people had a chance to make presidential history with Barack Obama, we backed our brother until the wheels fell off.

Yet when we had a chance to make history with Hillary, white women sidestepped our beloved Caucasian sister and welded those wheels of burden back on us. But it is clear to see through the glass slipper of data that this shoe doesn't fit on black people's feet; 90 percent of black people voted for Hillary Clinton. While white women, who are the largest group of voters, turned their backs on little girls all over the globe, for a demagogue. Cinderella must do better.

If we study American history, we should never be shocked or surprised when groups of white men make terrible decisions on the behalf of the rest of our nation. White male scholars got together and decided that a black person was three-fifths of a human being. It was white men who got out of their beds, took their white sheets with them, and formed a group called the Ku Klux Klan.

Our history is filled with disproportionately unfair practices initiated by white men in America. The founding fathers set the foundation for our nation on some uneven premises. All men can't be free and equal while some are enslaved.

This storm was built on imperfect pillars. The reason we keep replicating our nation's mistakes is because we try to avoid what we all know is the truth. The white church has all too often been a platform that hides hate in plain sight. All we need to do is go back on the time line to see why some whites felt the need to create so-called Christian academies; it is easy to see precisely when the rush to grab kids out of public schools for private church-based Christian academies occurred.

The Southern Education Foundation reports that from 1950 to 1965, private school enrollment grew at unprecedented rates all over the nation, with the South having the largest growth. By 1958, the South's private school enrollment had increased by more than a quarter of a million students, in those initial transitional first eight years of integration. Then the south boosted up to almost a million students in 1965.

Now let's parallel those findings with the historical timeline. The timeline leaves a trail of bread crumbs to easily conclude that folks fled public schools trying to hide their faith of hate in those newly formed private Christian academies.

In 1954, the Supreme Court handed down *Brown vs the Board of Education*, which declared that racially segregated public schools were unconstitutional. About the same time, there was a mass exodus of students taken out of public schools and sent to private Christian academies. Those parents should've known that is not Christlike.

Let's continue to stay with the timeline, which clarifies the deep sinister correlation. In 1957, nine students led by NAACP president Daisy Bates integrated Little Rock Central High School. The Little Rock Nine, as they were called, were Elizabeth Eckford, Minnijean Brown-Trickey,

Carlotta Walls LaNier, Melba Pattillo Beals, Thelma Mothershed Wair, Gloria Ray Karlmark, Ernest Green, Jefferson Thomas, and Terrence Roberts.

Those students were courageous catalysts who catapulted our society toward desegregated schools. They were only fourteen, fifteen, and sixteen years old. They also had skin like polished bronze and hair like a lamb's wool; plus, they put their lives on the line as a sacrifice for us. I'm not sure if those private Christian Academies are reading from the same bible that we read, but those brave black children are the ones who acted more like Christ!

History displays patterns we must learn from, that is, if we don't want to repeat those same mistakes. It is hard for enlightened minds to understand, why aren't our children taught about these valuable lessons in our public schools? My wife and I were fortunate enough to take our children on a pilgrimage to Little Rock to learn about our sacred American history.

I was definitely inspired to go after I sat through one of the most racially insulting history lessons I've ever heard at my child's Bear Creek Middle School in Statham.

The lecture was on the Civil War. And the history teacher, Mr. Kendrick's documented stance on the war was "I won't disclose how I personally feel about the war, because it's so political. I had relatives who fought on both sides of the war." In contrast MLK said in a 1967 sermon, "There comes a time where silence is betrayal."

More than 160 years after the start of the Civil War, it is an absolute betrayal to the educational process to teach this subject from a neutral political perspective. Enough time has passed, and there is plenty of factual information out there for Mr. Kendrick to draw some clear conclusions that should've led us to some fact-based learning on that day.

We teach students to speak up the moment when they see or experience something wrong. Yet Mr. Kendrick has had 160 years, and he is standing in front of those students teaching that he still can't make up his mind on how he feels about slavery! It is hypocritically irresponsible to frame historical facts as political. His stance, or his lack thereof one, is a perspective rooted in privilege hiding under a cloud of neutrality in plain sight.

In the hallway leading to Mr. Kendrick's class room was an image of a Negro riding on Abraham Lincoln's shoulders. While holding the Negro up, Lincoln was balancing on a tightrope. I took pictures of the image, because I noticed the Negro had been made to look like a monkey.

Mr. Kendrick then gave a lecture on how enormous the toll war was on Lincoln and all the good white people in the South. He told us Lincoln aged quickly because the war was so hard on him, and Kendrick said it was hard on his family too. This teacher of American history told us that his personal family lost hundreds of acres because they no longer had anyone to work them—for free.

Kendrick's last slide was a photo of his uncle's grave and the Confederate flag planted in it. He ended his lecture with "I was told my uncle was a handsome young man who didn't die from the injuries sustained to his neck during the Civil War. My dear uncle died because he was such a handsome young man that a nurse took a liking to him and baked him a pumpkin pie. The pie had seeds in it that infected my uncle's neck wounds, and he died from that infection."

In school nearly half a century ago, I heard the same misguided ideologies that I heard recirculating in Kendrick's 2019 classroom. I expressed my needed perspective to the school's Principal and to all of the white teachers who had sat through the same bland history lesson that I just had.

When addressing the sensitive subject of race, I learned from reading Dr. Ibram Kendi's book *Stamped, Racism, Antiracism, and You,* to ask everyone to take a deep breath when the topic becomes too uncomfortable. So, I suggested the breathing exercise to our seasoned group of educators.

Doing this simple exercise is useful in allowing truthful information to bypass the emotional response center of our amygdala, affording the facts time to reach our prefrontal cortex or the logical part of our brains.

Breathing is an undervalued tool in professional diverse environments to avoid the perpetual fight or flight. Or as Professor Robin DiAngelo describes the reoccurring obstruction hindering our needed racial conversations, *White Fragility*. White Fragility is another great book I've used as a learning tool, and I personally suggested it, as recommended reading, to what I had thought was a seasoned group of mature educators.

Therefore, I asked them, how do you think black and brown children will see themselves in this history lesson being taught like this mega mess in a modern-day classroom? As usual the clan of educators joined in white solidarity, rather than to embrace the chance to learn and hear from a diverse perspective.

It was a more comfortable response for those white women to bite their breaths, turn all red in the face, just to unanimously focus their discomfort with the truth, and their inherent distain onto me, for dare sharing it! As mature professional educators we must be able to take a deep breath, listen to learn rather than just listening to react and respond.

That way we can learn from other perspectives as it is our challenge to teach a diverse group of students from a myriad of backgrounds. I want to believe that the devastating subliminal messages Mr. Kendrick passed on were unintentional, but intentional or not, we can't keep feeding children pies with no seeds of truth placed in them. The long-term effects of these distortions of our history are even worse on white children.

For example, an older gentleman who works for the City of Statham has a Honda Civic, of which, it is sad that I have to say this, is a Japanese vehicle. Although some of the cars' and parts are outsourced for production in North America. The man's Civic is painted bumper to bumper with the Confederate flag, which symbolizes southerners' treasonous attempt to separate from the United States.

The Rebel Civic is parked in the middle of town for all to see every day. The gentleman tried to explain to me that anyone who doesn't see things the way he does is not a patriot. I realized halfway through the conversation that it's difficult to convince a grown man that everything he was taught as a kid was inaccurate, especially when the poor guy believed his Honda Civic was not a foreign vehicle, because he said and I quote "the car salesman told him Honda means American made!"

As southern hip-hop sensation and rapper TI said, "How dare I speak peace to a maniac?" In the South, all we can do is try. We try because we understand that it is our society that has failed people like this gentle rebel in our town, we still cannot afford to throw him or his Honda Civic away!

This is why I found that picture of Lincoln carrying a disregarded Negro on his shoulders so problematic. We know the Negro did most of the work to build the wealth of this nation.

If we want to teach what really happened, an image of Negroes bearing the weight of our nation while trying to balance a tightrope would be a more accurate historical depiction. It's important to hear some empathetic gratitude for the enslaved instead of teaching children to glorify the oppressors.

Students need to learn about Harriet Tubman, Frederick Douglass, and John Brown's stances against the injustices that started the Civil War. I cannot understand how an educator could say, "I have read Abraham Lincoln's writings, yet I try not to teach how I personally feel about the Civil War, because it is so political."

When what Lincoln wrote was, "We cannot survive as a nation half free and half slave." In school, lectures need to mention the sacrifices and contributions of the many people who were on the right side of history.

Our nation's great holocaust should not be taught to children as political but, rather, in its proper context as the inhumane and unequivocally wrong institution that it was. If our history is not taught truthfully, we lose a chance to learn from our mistakes.

I engaged Kendrick days after his lecture to give my feedback, because it is important to let leaders know when they are letting society down. You can do it in a nonconfrontational way if you ask the right questions. I asked him, "Mr. Kendrick, did you say that six hundred thousand soldiers died during the Civil War?"

"Yes," he said.

"How many of those soldiers that you counted were black?"

"None of them," he said.

I replied, "Kevin Hart is a comedian who released the *Guide to Black History* on Netflix, and Kevin noted that one hundred eighty-nine thousand black and brown soldiers died in the Civil War too. Are they any less dead? Were the lives they sacrificed any less valuable than those of the white soldiers' lives who you did mention in your history lesson?"

To his credit, he said no to both questions.

I responded, "Then why aren't their lives valued in your lesson plan?"

Mr. Kendrick turned as red as that Confederate Honda Civic parked in the middle of town!

I ended with "I don't expect a history teacher to have to jump onstage to inject some comedic wisdom into Kevin Hart's stage act. That is why I think it is unfair for Kevin Hart to have to come all the way South to inject some racially inclusive history into your history class."

There would be no need for African American History Month if we taught accurate American history all year!

This level of regurgitated ignorance requires a perfect storm, starting with parents blowing hurricanes of hot winds of misinformation to their children at home, in their huts. After that, our educational system recirculates those corrosive rains, showering down false beliefs onto the masses of formative minds in our kids' schools.

From home and school those wicked beliefs are being baptized by our culture every sunny day. Then those same sinister sentiments are ordained in networks of racist ideologies in churches every Sunday.

Ordained sentiments of supremacy, now feel emboldened to circulate in our communities and rain down with devastating effects on our society. This vicious cycle keeps our citizenry so confused that we have to debate on whether a Japanese car is American made! Racism reinvents itself, and people of color bear the pressure of its knees on our necks every day.

Our mother was relieved when she saw that police officer Derek Chauvin was convicted of murder. No, the verdict didn't bring back her brother who had been killed by the police, but it does at least say to the world that black lives matter.

The arc of moral justice is long, but it does bend toward justice. However, we have to pull like hell to get that arc to bend; simply complaining about it will not suffice. To achieve progress, we must pull on the arc as if our lives depend on it, because our lives actually do.

Accurate information is like flotation devices that allows our lives to survive these treacherous waters of America. In keeping our minds above these bubbling muddy ponds, we must be clear on who is tossing us floats of accurate information.

Reverend Al Sharpton said that President Obama was trying to do good works, but the talking heads on Fox News couldn't see anything the president was doing right. Fox News had a fit about a black man in a tan suit. I bet if those talking heads saw that a it was a bronze man walking on water, Sean Hannity would probably say, "Look at him! That Negro can't even swim."

A major cause of our disconnectedness in the South is fear. People can become frightfully delusional; historically they have made some of the worst decisions based on their unjustified unrest. The original silent film *Birth of a Nation* played on those imaginary apprehensions by portraying a black man as a savage whose sole reason for living was to rape white women. The story was a cinematic myth, but the movie's devastating effects are real.

That movie was a powerful pairing of the internal angst of white men with a cinematic representation on the big screen. *Birth of a Nation*'s reach was broad in society. It was even shown at the White House for the president at that time. The film is credited as the source that inspired the revitalization of the Ku Klux Klan on Stone Mountain in Georgia. The mere paranoid suspicions of a black man questing for the virtue of a white woman has gotten many black men killed.

Evil politicians manipulate these triggers and exploit them for political gain. President Bush Sr. used a Willie Horton ad to pave his path to becoming our president. Willie Horton was convicted of raping a white woman on a weekend pass while incarcerated in Massachusetts.

Eerily, Ronald Reagan chose to exploit those same worst corners of our political landscape by kicking off his candidacy in the infamous

Philadelphia, Mississippi, where a black man and two Jewish social workers were killed for registering citizens to vote. (Rest in power, James Chaney, Andrew Goodman, and Michael Schwerner.)

Political candidates often use this southern strategy as a way to manipulatively stoke anxieties to divert energy away from the logical parts of our brains. These appeals to fears keep our society spiraling in a perpetual cycle of fight-or-flight. Politicians exploit pathos arguments for political gain.

There are always three types of debaters in the barbershop: ethos, pathos, and logos. You'll find those same three types of reasoners outside our community as well. Being mindful of the patterns helps us recognize each type when we encounter it.

Ethos communicators talk as if being in the vicinity of something makes them an authority on it. For instance, ethos arguments start off a conversation like this: "I'm a police officer, my relative works in law enforcement, and my neighbor's cousin worked near the district attorney's office." In using that ethos introduction, people hope that whatever comes out of their mouths next is considered validated by the ethics or credibility of the person making the statement.

While it is unreasonable to think that it's okay to kill a black man for selling CDs just because your mama's cousin was a police officer, the ethical appeal is sometimes effective in clouding the logic. Gregory McMichael used his former employment at the DA's office to initially avoid getting him and his son Travis McMichael arrested for murdering Ahmaud Arbery.

Ethos arguments can lead to errors, but pathos arguments set the stage for the worst decisions ever made. Pathos discussions are based on emotions, such as fear. In 2008, when Obama was elected president, there was an unsubstantiated but pervasive fear all over the South that the black bogeyman was going to take all of our guns, and many went to gun stores and bought every gun in sight.

You couldn't even find a good water pistol anywhere. In contrast, Obama expanded gun rights by allowing citizens to have guns at national parks. It's like KRS-One said in "Step into a World (Rapture's Delight)":

"Steady packin' a gat as if something's gonna happen. But it doesn't, they wind up shootin' they cousin, they buggin'." Fear-inspired decisions can lead to bad results.

Most of the time, logos is the best method for reasoning because it means we are basing our decisions on facts, logic, or deductive reasoning. Logos discussions are useful ways to formulate accurate postulates. Appeals to logic are the most effective means to get a valid point across— that is, if you are having a discussion with open minds and reasonable ears.

MLK said that the two most dangerous things were sincere ignorance and conscientious stupidity. Sincere ignorance we understand because it means simply that someone doesn't know any better. Those who are conscientiously stupid, know better but choose to act as if they don't.

Let us again revisit the old southern saying that explains conscientious stupidity like this: "The man who cannot see is really not the blindest. The man who chooses not to see is."

Our founding fathers wrote in the Declaration of Independence that all men are created equal and endowed with the right to life, liberty, and the pursuit of happiness. However, at the same time, our founding fathers owned people as their property.

For God's sake, Thomas Jefferson kept his underage sister-in-law in a dungeon as his sex slave! One can't truly believe in freedom for all while holding over six hundred people captive. There is no logical connection between those two polar-opposite ideologies. Our founding fathers were the blindest because they wrote good things down on paper while pretending not to see the carnage of their own corruption.

Thomas Jefferson was a wealthy and powerful forty-year-old man who raped his wife's twelve-year-old sister and kept her in a dungeon for years, and we have his face carved on a mountaintop. Yet daily, some inner-city artist is arrested for spray-painting a picture of someone like John Lewis on the side of a moldy brick wall.

That is just another example of how we penalize poverty in America. If you go to court poor, you may never come out the same. Rest in peace, dear brother Kalief Browder.

In addition, small towns must become more conscious of the effects that environmental injustices can have on our communities. In 1999, Randolph Rainwater, an eleven-year-old boy, was killed when he fell into an illegally dug and unfenced sewage pit in our predominantly black area in Statham.

After Randolph's tragic death, Walter Hillman helped to start the Rainwater Foundation, whose purpose was to provide a safe place for our children to play. Later, the park was renamed to honor Hillman too. In Hillman Rainwater Park, I was fortunate enough to be part of an afternoon tutoring program provided by Demarcus, Hillman's son.

While acknowledging how far we still have to go, it is amazing when you think about how far we have come. The first president my son saw looked like him in a tan suit. When I was small if you put on a tan suit all you could expect to be was a peanut butter pastor!

Our son also wanted to play T-ball for Statham Little League, but I had my reservations because the same simpleminded family who had discouraged me as a youth from playing baseball was still involved in the Little League.

While I was reluctant, I looked into the league and saw there was a position available for a coach, so I took it. Mind you that this was before my activism got me blackballed from the league. I thought if I was a coach, I could change the culture to protect our children from some of the ignorance my generation endured as kids.

Boy was I wrong. All the other coaches at the first coaches' meeting were white. However, there was a black umpire there, whom I knew well.

When I got out of my car, the black umpire yelled out in front of everyone jokingly, "Uh-oh! Here comes the NAACP! What did we do wrong now?" I knew the brother's intent was sarcasm, but his outburst gave the white leaders the justification they needed to falsely label me as a troublemaker and put a target on my team's back for the rest of the season.

In that meeting, Mike, the president of Statham Little League, said, "I have bags and equipment for all the coaches." He pointed to one coach and said, "Sir, this is your bag." He pointed to another and another and told them the same thing while addressing them as *mister*, *sir*, and *Coach*. However, when he got to me, he said, "Here's your bag Bubba."

"Bubba?" I asked.

"Don't mind me," he said. "I call everybody Bubba."

"No sir Mike, you did not. You called every other coach here *mister*, *sir*, or *Coach*, but when you got to me, you called me Bubba."

Mike couldn't understand why I took offense to a random white man feeling entitled enough to just give me a name, so I tried to enlighten him. "Mike not too many years ago, your ancestors changed my ancestors' names without their input. Do you think that was right back then?" Even though we were playing baseball, I was sure that was a softball question. I waited in hopes that Mike would just say no, so I could show him that if a practice was wrong in 1614, then we should all understand that the practice is wrong more than four hundred years later.

Mike couldn't come up with an intelligent, coherent response. Therefore, I gave up on waiting and proceeded with my next questions. "Mike, what would make you think it is your privilege to issue out names to black men in these times?"

Mike showed an inability to respond to another simple question again.

"Sir," I said, "we are teaching kids more than just baseball. Baseball is a metaphor for life. And we don't want to reproduce children who will one day become men who think it's their privilege to walk up to some black man they don't know and give him a random name like Bubba. That's unacceptable in the twenty-first century."

I saw that Mike still didn't want to get it. He didn't feel the need to try to understand my perspective. You see privilege made Mike the president of the league in a faded pair of Wrangler jeans, while my son had to put on a full tan suit to look presidential.

The season didn't get any better after that initial meeting. Mike influenced the officials to make bad calls during our games. I kept a cool head about it because I wanted to set the right example for the kids. Frankly I didn't care if we won or not, just as long as the kids were having fun.

However, during one game, Mike was hanging around our dugout for no particular reason. It started pouring down raining, and my wife—the team mom—gathered the team and our daughter in our dugout for shelter.

Mike ran over and said, "Hey your daughter can't be in your dugout, because she's not on your team."

"Mike" I said, "my daughter's nine. Her mother is in there. Her brother is in there. I'm her father. If a nine-year-old girl is not with one or both of her parents in the rain, where do you think she is supposed to be? Better yet Mike, look at the other dugout. It looks like Noah's Ark over there."

There were about forty people, two cats, two dogs, and what looked like a giraffe in the other dugout, because even a giraffe knows it just makes good sense to seek shelter in the rain!

After I made Mike aware that he was using standards for my team that differed from those he was applying for the other team, he pulled his Wranglers up and said, "Heck, I'm about to go over there to see if those forty people and that giraffe are on the other team Bubba!"

Mike left us alone for the rest of that game, but I knew that before the season ended, he would be back. Some folks down south don't like it when you refuse to become the shrinking Negro they have become accustomed to knowing. I threw Mike off by not giving in to his microaggression of being called Bubba. And that snowballed into Mike aggressively thinking I was going to put my precious daughter out in the rain. The Mikes of the world truly believe that black men have no rights a white man is bound to respect.

Therefore, I wrote a scathing red letter to the baseball board, complaining about the situation. I added to my complaint the public-safety issue of having no access to running water at the field and having just one fumed-up porta-potty that could be smelled from miles away.

Everyone knew the conditions were unsafe with no running water, especially since our teams met in the middle of the field after each game for high fives. Then, postgame, each team of children met at our fly-infested concession stand to dine with no running water.

Not one board member responded to my letter addressing these concerns about the safety of our children, so I sent the same scathing red letter to our newspaper, which ran it as a letter to the editor.

Apparently, someone in our public health department read my complaint about high fives and food from the concession stand, with no running water to wash. I was later told the health department determined we had prime conditions for an outbreak of the *E. coli* virus, and they came and shut down the concession stand, finding the place unfit to serve food.

Before our team's next game, every board member who had refused to address my concerns privately, desperately sought to contact me now. I pulled up to the field and saw the health department had boarded up the concession stand like it had been hit by Hurricane Katrina. An angry mob of people approached my vehicle with steam pouring out of their ears. Mike was leading the pack. He asked me, "Coach why did you close the concession stand down?"

I calmly replied, "Surely you don't think I would close the concession stand down? Shoot I love those hot dogs too."

"Barnard but you wrote that letter to the newspaper!"

I replied "No sir! No way. You're wrong. I didn't write no letter to the newspaper."

Mike asked, "So who wrote that letter then Coach Barnard?"

Finally, I replied, "Bubba did. It was Bubba who wrote that letter to the editor."

If looks could kill, I would probably be dead. Anytime a black man responds to ignorance with tact, it seems to drive some folks even crazier. We have to always try to respond with tactful purpose, because as my uncle Johnny taught me, if a fool and a wise man are in the middle of town fighting, people walking by will not know the difference. Observers walking by will just think they see two fools fighting. Therefore, we have to be wise and respond with compassionate tact.

After that, the angry mob got so mad that they made up a story claiming that I had cursed out some white woman I had never even seen before. Yet as a black man, it is almost impossible to be believed, especially when dealing with the likes of a *Karen*.

Thankfully those lies didn't escalate to a made-up rape. Now that sounds extreme to some, but if you are dipped into the chocolate nuances of American history, you completely understand that that is the, go-to, lie typically told when people really want to get rid of a black man. The extremes folks will go through to try to get you to shrink are without limits.

After the conjured-up accusation, for no reason, the board kicked me out of the league with the assistance of two Barrow County deputies, who escorted me off the premises. The saddest part is that this all took place in front of our crying T-ball team—all five- and six-year-old kids.

The one thing that gave me hope was a white grandmother whose granddaughter was on my team; she was furious! I must have made a positive impression on them, because the grandmother had never said a word before (because she didn't have many teeth), but when the police started escorting me off the premises, the enraged grandmother yelled, "Coach Barnard ain't never done nothing to nobody!"

I never thought I'd be so happy to see such a mad white woman in my life. Her gesture taught me that by speaking up, you can be the conduit to cure the silently complicit. We can never give up on humanity. There are allies and accomplices waiting to be called out of the woods, because the harvest is plenty.

After further investigation we found out that according to the official league handbook, the board had kicked me out of the league without due process. I guess the board members should've read the handbook they were supposed to abide by. When the officials found out they were supposed to notify me in writing and have a hearing to hear my denial of the made-up accusation, the board began to scramble backwards trying to cover up their errored mistake.

Johnny Smith, my mentor from the NAACP, came to the meeting with me and told the Little League board, "We're going to sue all of you. Y'all didn't give Coach Barnard his due process. We are going to sue to take all the baseballs, bats, and bases, and Coach Barnard is going to put a double-wide trailer out here right behind second base, and his children are going to be able to play baseball out here anytime they want to!"

I had to hold my breath to keep from laughing at my mentor in the movement, Johnny Smith. It is always reassuring to know someone has your back, but he didn't have to tell the Little League board we were going to sue for all the baseballs and bats! United though through the revelation of the dream, we can level out any playing field.

Often, we will hear the complainers, who just watch from the sidelines, say things like "You're better than me!" What they are really implying is that activists are fools for even trying to make things better, which is a mistake, because not all people are unreasonable.

Of course, we do understand that the folks who stormed the Capitol Building and pooped in their britches just to wipe their feces on the walls of Congress, they may be just a wee bit beyond reason's reach. However, they're not the ones I'm talking about here. The people we can reach are waiting for us to take the lead on the issues that most affect us. But if we aren't willing to speak up for ourselves, we cannot expect other people to stand with us.

The second mistake people in the complainers' club make is, thinking that cussing folks out is a productive solution. Really? What has cussing folks out ever done except give a brief moment of personal satisfaction? Name one law that was changed simply because someone got cussed out? Ida B. Wells, Frederick Douglass, and MLK didn't make history by cussing folks out. We don't celebrate a national MLK cuss folks out holiday! I am certain they wanted to cuss some folks out at times, but those catalysts completely understood the big picture.

I learn lessons every day simply by listening to the elders in the barbershop. And I have also learned lessons the hard way when I didn't listen to learn. I was taught in executive leadership training through the NAACP to never go alone to meetings with public officials.

The reasoning being rooted in the reality that in America it is so hard for a black man to be believed. If you are alone and the enemy makes up a story, we catch hell in trying to prove that white lies are still untrue. That is a harsh reality all activist must understand. Sadly, it is a truth that is baked into the nature of our nation's DNA. Carolyn Bryant told a lie on Emmett Till in 1955, and she's still living. While Mamie Till's only, fourteen year old, son has been dead since then.

See how Marcus Garvey was painted as a demagogue even in the black community for simply encouraging a sense of self-pride and self-worth in us?

And Malcolm X is still portrayed as a violent extremist for being cornered into self-defense. The image of Malcolm standing guard with a shotgun at his daughter's bedroom window, after he had been firebombed by terrorist, is still misunderstood as violent imagery instead of self-defense. I hear brothers say all the time in the barbershop, "I'm more Malcom than Martin," without understanding that being compared to either martyr would be the utmost compliment.

Malcolm X did not commit any violent acts against anyone after he joined the Nation of Islam, but the image of Malcolm X with a gun has been sensationalized and has become propaganda to overlook the fact that he was just a father trying to protect his young girls in his home.

In this world, the victims of violence are made to appear to be violent themselves. These subliminal messages influence our consciousness into justifying black deaths. These misrepresentations make us believe that pigmented people are somehow inherently dangerous, leading society to preconceive that we get what we deserve.

I heard on *The Joe Madison Show* that 90 percent of the churches in the South didn't want MLK to come to their churches, because they perceived that he was the one causing the problems in the South. That notion sounds ridiculous today, but at the time, with the way the media covered him, that 90 percent figure is not hard to believe.

King was labeled a trouble making Communist for simply pointing out the problems in this country. Knowing that history helps us to understand why we are trained to always travel in at least twos. For we know that it is easy for untruthful people to discredit one honorable person of color.

One afternoon, I mistakenly thought I could bypass this rule and go alone to the Barrow County's sheriff's office to pick up an open records request for the NAACP. That error in judgment could have easily cost me my life. I was following up on a few complaints about the abuse of inmates by deputies in Barrow County's detention center, and I submitted a records request with Kimberly Phillips, the records manager, at that time.

Phillips called me and told me the records I had requested were ready for me to pick up. I mistakenly told Phillips I was already in Winder and would be right by for the records. I should've known something wasn't right, because my requests for public records were never responded to that fast, if at all. Therefore, I rushed to get to the sheriff's office; I wanted to see this miracle for myself.

When I arrived at the old courthouse used as the sheriff's office, I told Phillips I was there to retrieve the open records, and she called someone. As I was waiting, Jamie, one of the few black deputies at the sheriff's office, mysteriously appeared. I knew him well because I was his barber. He and I chatted for a while, and then I noticed that the fully staffed sheriff's office had dwindled down to just the records manager, Deputy Jamie, and me.

I thought, *Wow, it's taking an extremely long time to get the records that Phillips told me were already ready.*

At that moment, Chief Deputy Colonel Jimmy Lomax and Major Mike Katsegianes from the detention center came bursting through the courthouse doors as mad as a mob. Lomax was dressed as if he had just rushed from the farm; he was wearing a plaid shirt, Wranglers, cowboy boots, and a belt buckle so big that it looked like the belt Ric Flair won from Harley Race in the Wrestling Championship.

Katsegianes seemed to be the most enraged by my presence. You see, my request exposed that the same deputy, under the direction of Katsegianes, was involved in a pattern of abuse of inmates, according to the records I had requested. The only professional option the sheriff's office knew was to try to bully and intimidate the activists, rather than working with us to better serve and protect the public.

Katsegianes had a nervous twitch. And he kept fidgeting and directing his voice toward the records manager's office without an ounce of provocation from me. I was more than ten feet away from him, but he yelled at me, "Get your hand out of my face!"

I looked over and saw Phillips self-obstructing her own line of vision by hiding behind her office door. At that moment, I realized this situation was serious. I had made the mistake of abandoning my training to go alone, putting my fate in the hands of people dressed up as public safety officers.

It is a mistake I will never make again. Not even in broad daylight on Broad Street can you trust going to the sheriff's office alone! If anything had happened to me that day, it would have been my word against the word of the three officers—if I had been lucky enough to have a word at all. The brother who had stalled me all that time, Jamie, had strangely vanished into the thin southern air.

Phillips was setting the stage to be able to say she hadn't seen anything because she was shielded by her office door. However, she could say she had heard Katsegianes yell at me to get my hand out of his face. When in truth, Shaquille O'Neal wouldn't have been able to put his hand in the man's face, considering I was well over ten feet away from him.

Nervously, I projected my voice back at the half hiding Phillips, "Don't worry about my records request! I'm walking away!"

Katsegianes barked, "Don't walk away from me!"

I replied, directing my voice again towards Phillips, "I'm walking away from you now Major! Remember that in your report Ms. Phillips. Have a nice day." I cautiously left the premises, payed for by the public. I am blessed to be able to give this accurate account of our public safety officials with no professional standards at all.

It is very disappointing when you witness first-hand how our publicly funded entity can operate with a manner of such desperate corruption. Our government was designed to function with transparency and openness. The powers that we the people give to elected officials who serve us with dark and sinister motives is shameful.

We teach our children how wrong bullying is, but then we elect leaders at our sheriff's office who are just bullies in blue. If I was the sheriff like Jud Smith is, I would have the decency to be ashamed. Trump was a bully in chief, and his attitude trickled all the way down to these rural local leaders.

The flowing of these aggressive attitudes are ones that citizens face every day in America from supposed peace officers. Since that day, I have sent several formal complaints to the sheriff's office that were never, to a moral ethical professional standard, properly addressed.

All this means though is that we activist need to maintain our connections, for our protection. Especially in the South, we have to band together. Our survival requires us to depend on one another.

That was not the only time when those bullies in blue tried to silence me. Thank God for training through connecting with a network of activists all across the South; they've helped me learn how to deal with the bullies in blue. Activist training also taught us to expect the enemy to want you quiet, especially when you're sharing truths that the wicked want to keep unknown.

Networking with other activists gives you more peace in knowing that even the smallest towns are still connected to the rest of the world. Just as our grandmas would sew small pieces of fabric together into a blanket to keep us warm all winter, we can consider ourselves valued patches in the larger fabric of the universe.

On another occasion, Mr. Johnny Smith and I went to the sheriff's office to complain about a sergeant's and a captain's comments on Facebook. We were concerned that Sergeant David Aderhold made some comments so threatening about President Obama that the US Secret Service came to pay our small-town sergeant a personal down-home visit.

I asked Sheriff Smith, "How can a man who has taken an oath to serve and protect the citizens of America, then go on Facebook and threaten the President of the United States of America, still be entrusted to serve and protect me?"

Sheriff Smith sat in silence. Silence speaks volumes, because we know silence is complicity.

We also questioned Captain Lewis Rusgrove's posts in which he called President Obama "a camel jockey" and referred to African Americans backing the president as "Damocrats, gays, baby killers, and potheads." Our meeting with the sheriff ended with him saying, "You guys aren't going to tell me how to run my sheriff's office."

We said okay and then we used the tools God has given us to shine a bit of light into these dark rural spaces. I emailed Monica Pearson of WSB Channel 2 News about the incident, and I got a call from reporter Kerry Kavanaugh. She interviewed me in front of the sheriff's office. A few hours after the captain's racially insensitive comments made the national news, he resigned in lieu of being terminated. I posted this story on YouTube under "Barrow Captain Resigns."

We might not be able to tell a sheriff or any other leader how to run his or her office, but MLK told us, "The arc of the moral universe is long, but it bends toward justice." The moral universe is no one man's office. The universe belongs to the almighty God. You are made in God's image. Therefore, the Almighty will help you guide the universe into bending it in the righteous way.

Attempts to intimidate activists with lies and slander are inevitable; they come with the territory. Through our activist training we learn to expect the unexpected. We should also realize that in rural America, hair salons are important points for transformational information. In the barbershop, there is always and elder trying to give the young'uns some game.

In the beauty salon, there is always someone sharing important information about a school board or a critical county commissioners' meeting. Our communities are less connected without these pivotal informational centers planted almost everywhere we go.

The issues that disproportionately affect black and brown communities are often ignored by overwhelmingly Republican districts' press. Therefore, about ten years ago, I decided to transition the needed dialogue from the barbershop into a weekly, hour-long radio show.

The Way It Is, was my way to disperse accurate information about important issues concerning our community, to our community. I was inspired by Joe Madison's daily radio show question: "What are you going to do about it?"

And this is what I did. We had local entrepreneurs on the show, and we solicited politicians, educators, health-care experts, and survivors of abuse, as well as local artists and activist.

Since then, many in our rural community have started their own live shows today, which is great if one understands the responsibility of public speech. I have always heard, "Boy don't you open your mouth unless you have something to say." If you are starting a podcast for personal publicity, that's cool.

In contrast, our effort, on "The Way It Is" was to give a voice to the voiceless.

We've all seen football players run into the end zone acting as if he wants to congratulate the player who has just scored a touchdown, but when the camera comes on, there he is with his face right in the camera yelling, "Hi Mom!" When the lights are on, it's clear to see who's in it for the glory and who's in it to help share our story.

We have to ask ourselves, *what's my intention for speaking?* If we just talk about a popular person or clout chase someone who has died how does that information help our rural community? It takes little courage to speak about the ever-present injustice on the other side of the world, but what are you saying about the injustices that are happening at home in your own area code?

Rural pockets are places where you'll find pulpits full of spineless preachers, who lack the moral conviction to speak on the racial disparities of the flocks they pastor. It behooves me, trying to understand the point of ministers here?

When black men were being brutalized by the police, while incarcerated in the Barrow county jail, the only pastor who spoke at our rally said "we must pray for the police." I don't understand how a man of God would just pray for the oppressors and never mention the oppressed. When in my spiritual southern journey, I have learned from the elders that what we do for the least of these, in essence, is our divine servitude to God.

Plants grow where they are planted. Righteous indignation requires us to operate with compassion for the people placed where we grow.

Our pastors are timid because freedom of speech can be costly. People with the courage to speak the truth have a true calling—a costly calling that in our history had Hoover's FBI put out hits on our black leaders.

In 1969, Chairman Fred Hampton of the Black Panther Party was drugged and assassinated in his sleep by Chicago police, in coordination with the FBI, while in bed with his pregnant fiancée. Even now, in 2021, Hampton's tombstone in Louisiana gets riddled with bullets. It says something sinister that even a man who has been dead for fifty-two years still can't rest in peace.

Speech is supposed to be free right? What is easily proven is that, free speech can cost you your life. But if a man has not found that in which he is willing to die for then he is not fit to live.

Sugarcoating our conversations just to make others more comfortable is appeasement. Appeasement is the currency that supports white supremacy. We don't need another Clarence Thomas nor any more Herschel Walkers making daily deposits in America's banks of white supremacy. We need willing workers from all races to make some withdrawals from that account to tear down these evil structures.

As part of my NAACP work, I was the local liaison for Professor Janis McDonald, a professor of law at the University of Syracuse. McDonald was in Barrow County to gather information on suspicious unsolved deaths of black men in the South.

As the barber who had been in the area all my life, I was asked to tag along with the professor during interviews in the hope that people seeing my familiar face would make more citizens willing to talk. Being that I was the town barber, I humbly was the perfect fit! We uncovered many truths about past events.

It was as if my mere presence made it easy for citizens to talk. It was a gift I will never undervalue nor ever forget. Many find it easy to talk to a barber or beautician. People will tell you almost anything when you have a license to hold a straight razor to their throats! Seriously, though, most of the people we interviewed had felt some tragedies firsthand. Many of those traumas had been suppressed for years.

The Professor and I would go into a house to investigate one death, and we would hear about several other suspicious deaths before we could reach the door. As a black man who knows what it means to be black in America, I was still shocked to see how much pain our people had suppressed just to sustain their sanity. The research from that fieldwork let me know we have a lot more work to do.

Professor McDonald explained that if we cannot give suffering families the justice they deserve, we can only hope they will find some comfort in knowing that we care enough to try, because their loved ones' lives mattered too.

I was emotionally drained after interviewing Jane. With empathy, we felt the weight Jane had lived with for years as the last person to see my uncle Joe Charles Muckle alive, before he was taken into custody by the police. Jane spoke to us while wearing the present pain she had suppressed for more than sixty years.

Professor McDonald and I realized the burden of responsibility needed to be lifted from some of these survivors, because they were victims too. There was nothing the woman could have done to save my uncle from being killed by the police, but she kept saying she wished she could have done something to save him.

The Professor left me with these words of encouragement that still guide my quest for justice today. She said, "Barnard, some people ask, 'Why go through all this? Why would you put people through rehashing things that happened decades and even centuries ago?'"

She said the reason people thought it was okay to kill black people was because someone had taught them it was okay to get away with it before, back then. "We're doing God's work to correct the record for the future," she said. That's the mission that fuels our purpose today. We are not marginal or expendable. We were made in God's image. It is past time for our contributions and lives to be valued in our society as such.

We tried to pour those sentiments into our radio show, and I got the confirmation I needed. In our training, we were taught that we would know we were on the right tracks when people started calling us from jail and when the police tried to intimidate us into shutting up. I once got a call from someone in our county's detention center. I asked him, "How'd you get my number?"

The guy told me, "Barnard, an inmate wrote your number on a jail cell wall."

It is humbling to know that one isolated person in a lonely place knew that I was someone who cared. We can't help everybody, but we can help at least one person in need. If we all did just that, everyone in the world would feel covered, just like I felt under the warmth of my grandmas' blanket.

Professor McDonald also left me with wise instructions on what to do if strange things started to happen to me after she left town. She said it was normal for some people in rural areas to revert to their old ways of intimidation by terrorism. The obvious reason for their pathos-based aggression was directly related to our work in exposing truths they wanted unknown. We were asking questions that some townsfolk didn't want answered.

Over the next couple of days after our research, quite a few things happened. My car was stolen from right behind my back under my garage door as I waited on my children to come out of the house for church. Four days later, there was an attempt to break in at my mother's home.

The third incident I recorded and posted on YouTube called "Barnard's run in with Barrow police." A Barrow County officer kept creeping by my barbershop one October night while I was cleaning up. I saw the officer circling like a shark.

He turned onto my driveway and then quickly darted left onto my neighbors' grass. I pulled out my cell phone and started recording. Deputy Siple went through my neighbor's yard to approach my building from the back. As the deputy approached me, I already had both my hands up, while holding my phone, recording, over my head. I asked him, "Sir, can I help you?"

He started barking commands at me like a sick dog with Tourette's syndrome. "Put your phone down!"

"Why are you here? I asked. This is private property. Nobody's called you," I said.

Deputy Siple commanded me to get my hands out of my pockets, though the only two hands I have were already over my head. He commanded me to give him my driver's license. I told him I didn't have my license on me, because I wasn't driving. I was at home on my own property, almost seventy yards off of a rural road.

The deputy wanted me to explain to him why I was at my own home, though he had no warrant or call-in and no reason to be on my property. I told him I owned the place, thinking that would help the deputy understand my reason for being there.

In addition, the only car parked on my property came back registered in my name. In spite of those facts, the deputy called for backup and threatened to take me to jail. Black or white, you have every right to be at home.

When the officers he called for backup got there, they saw that I was recording what was happening and understood the circumstances better than the first deputy did. The Fourth Amendment states that we have a right to be secure on our own property. Without a crime committed, Deputy Siple had no probable cause to be suspicious of a crime.

But if those officers had not intervened, Deputy Siple would have taken me to jail for just simply being on my own property. Some would say I was in the wrong place at the wrong time. I disagree, because if a black man at home is in the wrong place, then where else is there left for us to go?

Even the esteemed black Harvard professor Henry Louis Gates was arrested at his own home in Cambridge, Massachusetts. My testimonies as a black man are not isolated incidents. Racial profiling of black and brown Americans is a part of life we have to learn to deal with, until we change the things we can no longer accept.

In spite of the realities, we find comfort in knowing we are all connected; we are not alone. We must lift our voices as high as the listening skies, because God is listening. As David took a smooth stone to take down Goliath, we must take our truths and toss them at the universe.

I see podcasters from all over using their platforms to communicate our truths to the masses. We need more books, letters to the editors, and talk radio shows from out of the sticks. *Out da Sticks Productions* produced my first radio show. In my humble opinion, we did well for a radio show coming from a rural area code.

We are inspired by voices like Ice Cube. A brother from the streets of Compton created a document called the Contract with Black America. Cube's CWBA addresses the wealth gap that has plagued America for years. Black Americans are nearly 14 percent of the population yet have only 0.5 percent of the nation's wealth.

Ice Cube thinks we should have at least 14 percent of the wealth, considering this country was built on our ancestors' backs. It took centuries of orchestrated terrorism to create this wealth gap. It shouldn't take nearly that long to correct the disparities, if we put forth some effort. Our task is to recognize the brilliance in us. We have to invest in one another if we expect the rest of the nation to.

Cube also wrote and produced the movie *Barbershop* and its sequel. In most black communities, you learn a lot at the barbershop. There is almost always someone in the shop who thinks he knows everything.

Oddly enough, those who talk the most think they are right just for being loud. It's as if volume is the litmus test for correctness. In our barbershops and beauty salons, enlightened minds from every walk of life meet and learn from each other. The key is to discern whom we should be listening to.

A wise man in the barbershop told us this story. One day an electrician, a physician, and an attorney were in the shop at the same time. While the barber was cutting the doctor's hair, a tree fell on a power line, triggering a power outage. Initially the barber told everyone in the salon, "Do not go out there near that tree!"

But the lawyer was in a hurry, so he rushed outside to pull the tree off of the power line. The lawyer grabbed the bottom of the tree, trying to move it off the electrically charged power line, without understanding that the tree had become a conductor for the electrical current looking for a place to ground. The lawyer was jolted by the current into an electrical freeze.

At that moment of emergency, the medical doctor instinctively jumped out of the barber's chair and ran out to the helpless lawyer's aid, when he too was contorted by a jolt of electricity.

The lawyer and the doctor were fidgeting around like Turbo and Ozone in the movie *Breakin' 2*. After a few moments, the tango was over, and the electrical current seemed to turn the two a loose.

Everyone in the salon was happy that the doctor and lawyer were okay. As the two came back into the barbershop, their hair was sticking straight up like Don King's. They got upset, wondering why the electrician hadn't gotten involved or said anything. The electrician responded, "I didn't need to say nothing! Hell, the barber told y'all don't go out there!' The moral of the story is you should always listen to your barber."

Barbers learn by listening to various wise people. Barbers also have platforms to be voices for our communities. We are pivotal points for critical information to be shared. It is our moral obligation to use our platforms for much more than just talking about one another.

I have always lived in small-town America; it's still a struggle to overcome the lack of opportunities in the rural South. However, on my journey, I am finding that we are not limited to just what we see. I read Charlamagne Tha God's book *Black Privilege* and realized that he too came from a dirt road. Now his voice has paved paths for our voices to connect with the rest of the world. You can be like Alexander Hamilton and write your way out.

You are an important piece in the fabric of the entire universe. A southern awakening will be your awakening call. The South has something to say through you. Now, rise up and say it! Saying something doesn't mean just complaining about what other activists aren't doing. Complaining without having an established record in activism played out hundreds of years ago.

No one remembers the Negro who was at the barbershop in 1862 complaining about what Frederick Douglass didn't do. However, we remember Frederick Douglass because his words became deeds that fit needs.

No one remembers the brother in a barbershop complaining because MLK didn't say anything about him in his Nobel Peace Prize speech. I can imagine there was a loud person in the barbershop in 1964 who said, "All I done for King, and he didn't say nothing about me in his speech. I was the one who shelled them pecans for Mama Carleen when she made that Negro a pecan pie!"

It sounds funny, but do you know of anyone who had a holiday named after him for just complaining? Therefore, what good is it to be a nonactivist going around town complaining about what other devoted activists are doing?

In addressing nonactivist complainers at the barbershop, I try to channel my inner Judge Judy by asking the clear questions to cut the chase. When I hear complainers say things like "See? Tamika Mallory and 'nem up there in jail for protesting the death of Breonna Taylor, and Tamika 'nem ain't say nothing about fixing the wheelchair ramp on my grandma's front porch."

"Mrs. Complainant," I say, "doesn't your grandma have sixteen grandsons who all have Harley-Davidsons?"

"Yes, bu—"

"That's enough! You've answered my question. Tell your grandma to get one of her sixteen grandsons to fix her ramp, put grandma on the back of their Harley Davidson, and ride grandma up that ramp to get her into her house.

Furthermore, Mrs. Complainant, don't you dare come back into my courtroom until your activism is as loud as your complaining. If you move in silence, don't complain out loud."

Likewise, if a bully steps on your toes in the South, you have every reason to scream. However, if all you are going to do is scream, get ready, because that bully might keep stepping on your toes. If you punch the bully in the mouth, he might stop stepping on toes completely.

We have to be willing to do more than just complain. Elevate your complaints to the point of action; and then apply some of those actions to your complaint. The action does not have to be hitting a bully in the mouth, but you do need to use your loud voice outside the comfort of the barbershop. We need to see that same volume mixed with righteous energy out in the community.

If you are not willing to do that, please shut up, and move on in silence. Real activists have real work to do besides arguing with you about doing nothing.

Actionable steps are easy to take today. You can download an app on your phone called 5 Calls. If you don't like something a legislator has approved for your community, no matter where you live, the 5 Calls app will connect you directly to that legislator, and you can talk with that person, leave a message, or send an email expressing your complaint. People who stop at just complaining in our community rarely reach positions of power.

My good friend Norman Garrett didn't like what was going on in his district, so he ran for the seat, and he won. Now Norman is in a position of power to do something about what we complain about. I solute my brother Norman Garrett, city councilman in Monroe, Georgia.

Postulate 4

HAIR COMES, HAIR GOES, AND NEGROES

"HAIR COMES, AND hair goes" is a concept I got from working with the nonprofit Leap for Literacy. Stan Tucker is its founder. Stan was having an event encouraging young people to tell their stories by becoming authors. During the event he asked me up onstage. He and I both shave our heads now.

As Stan was addressing a group of about eight hundred elementary students, He looked to me and said, "This man is still my barber even though I no longer have hair. My barber is here because he has always supported any positive thing that I was doing. My barber was at all my basketball games and most of my football games too."

In his book *Stan and the Man*, he shares his story of how he lost his father, as a kid, in a tragic accident. I relate to him well because my father died before he could validate me as a man as well. Young black boys can act out, seeking that manly validation. It was so moving for me to hear Stan's story and how a haircut intertwined with words of encouragement can help mold a boy into a man.

A great haircut can also boost one's self-esteem. Provided the service is given in a positive and uplifting atmosphere. Barbershops can also give our youth the encouragement they need to become the positive and productive members of our society that we need. Stan's kind words awakened me to the fact that hair comes and goes, but how we treat one another seeps through our minds, our hearts and our souls to shape our lives forever. Amen.

Now we have to address the elephant in the room: The *Negroes* part of this postulate's title. The Negro part can reach a brother's heart also but sometimes not in a good way. I have supported my clients and their kids in their activities for decades. The part that can become a nuisance to my spirit is a Negro like the following.

There once was a Negro mother not like the one referenced by the great poet Langston Hughes. The Negro mother I write about here had a son who played baseball. She was always giving me sob stories about how her son's father could never make it to the games.

All her complaints I'd heard before, and I imagined the kid was sad about continuously hearing his mother complaining about his father's absence too. Therefore, I closed my shop and went to the boy's game. The kid was excited when he saw me hanging over the fence watching him play. I had to remind him a few times to turn around and watch the field: "Kid, keep your eye on the ball!" But he didn't. The little boy was just too excited to see me there.

When the game was over, I congratulated him and said, "Son you played a great game!" It made me feel good to be in a position to be there for someone else.

The kid's mother kept bragging on me way too much, saying, "Barnard the Barber closed his shop to come see my son play ball!" It's uncomfortable to be bragged on too much, because to God be the glory in all we do. Secondly, you have to watch when people are hyping you up too much in your presence, because they are usually the same ones who will tear you down behind your back.

Less than a year later, she saw me being a dad at the same baseball field; I was watching my son play baseball. She asked me, "What are you doing here? We just came by your shop, and you were closed. My son needs a haircut. You need to be going back to open up the shop!"

The nerve of this type of Negro. When you are doing something for their kid, they are thrilled. But when you are doing something for your own child, the thrill is gone.

Barbers always have clients who want them to come in early, skip lunch, or stay late. Over time, this will stretch beauticians very thin. Clients tell me all the time, "Barnard, I've never seen you stop to eat lunch."

As we care for others, we must be mindful to also care for ourselves. Remember, you can't pour from an empty cup. Customers aren't often considerate of that, because we have been programmed to believe that customers are always right. Barbers and beauticians often abuse our health for the sake of our clients. Most of us do this without our clients ever hearing us complain. We are trained to listen to the struggles of others while suppressing and disregarding our own. We need to shift our mindsets to prioritize some time for ourselves.

The pandemic forced me to put the needs of my family first. It also cleared the space for me to realize that if I am not in a good place, there's not much positivity I'll have to share. Again, you cannot pour from an empty cup. Therefore, please don't let anyone make you feel bad about taking care of yourself. You must respect the time with your family, and make others respect that time as well.

My family use to go on our vacation once a year at Disney World in Florida. I would let all my clients know the dates I would be out of town, and that information was on my answering machine and on a sign in my window as well.

But there was always a customer who would call me, despite knowing I was on my vacation. My grandma used to call people like that educated fools. Educated fools have book sense but no common sense nor common courtesy. Before someone would leave for college, my grandma would secretly give them all the money she had saved up in her empty snuff can and say, "Now, don't you come back here no educated fool."

An educated fool is someone who goes to a school right down the road and comes back looking down on the same community that has supported them. Going down the road does not make one a Rhodes scholar.

There are some black folks who have wholeheartedly embraced European standards of enlightenment just to look down on their own culture. We need these prodigal sons and daughters to utilize their degrees to help lift our communities up, not to put us down.

The house Negro and the field Negro were both slaves who needed each other to survive. Education can be an equalizer if it is not used like our complexions, to divide our communities even further.

I'll bet you know someone who went off and came back only asking about the people they thought were doing worse than them? In the barbershop, there are brothers who come into the salon and give their credentials as if they are in my barber's chair for a job interview: "Yeah you know, I got two degrees. I got my bachelor's and my master's."

Some educated fools think we don't know the steps to obtaining degrees. At this pace, Negroes like this will finish up and get a PhD in what my grandma called educated foolishness.

Degrees without works in your community are just pieces of paper. Go to college to earn a degree in what you love, and when you come back, show your community some of that love.

If you climb a ladder, look around for ways to help others climb up that ladder too. I see too many in my town leave and never look back. It's almost as if they think they might turn into salt. We need you to come back to share with us what you've learned.

Invest just an hour a month in doing something positive for your community; everyone can engage in giving back. Remember those like my grandmother, who gave all she had from her empty snuff cup.

As a community college graduate, I am not minimizing the quality of enlightenment one can receive in college. But some Negroes who no one considered bright when they left town always comes back talking all bougie and upscale. I never understood that phenomenon.

They try to make themselves feel big by trying to make us feel small. It's like a grown man looking for a group of second graders to stand next to just to appear taller. Real growth is not about that.

Let us use our educations to lift one another up. The variations of our complexions—from light to dark—have historically been exploited to keep us from coming together. It is counterproductive for us to let our educations become our next great divide.

We are a village of descendants who need each other to survive, and we cannot quench our community's thirst with vinegar. Be educated enough to come back with buckets of water for your brothers and sisters. And In the words of my grandma, "don't you come back here no educated fool!"

My wife is an educated woman whose wisdom shines brightly, without her boasting about her degrees. I am just thankful that her distinctions have little bearing on who's making our Kool-Aid tonight. Her Kool-Aid magically turns water into wine. What a wonderful Negro mother!

The client I mentioned earlier with two degrees, called me during my family's Disney vacation because the other barber in our salon had charged him three dollars more than he usually paid me. But you do the math: three dollars for a man with two degrees should not be that big of a deal. Right? This is the educated foolishness we have to filter out of our community.

I've also had friends who've served in the military. They too will come back home asking the same kind of condescending questions: "Where's so-and-so? I bet he's in jail. Where's so-and-so? I bet he's still here in Statham." One close friend came back, after his third tour of duty in the desert, and said to me, "Boy I tell you, ain't nothing in Statham. You need to get out of here."

I replied, "No thanks man. I'm good here because ain't nothing in Iraq either. President George W. Bush didn't find any weapons of mass destruction. Y'all didn't even run into any mean German shepherds over there. Heck man, when you were in Iraq, General Colin Powell couldn't even show us one WAP". For those of you who don't know, WAP is an acronym for a Wet-Ass water Pistol.

Anyway, thankfully the soldier is my good friend. And he knows I would never disrespect the sacrifices he made to serve our nation. In fact, he thought my joke was the funniest. He said, "After all I've been through, it's good to be back home in the barbershop! I needed a good laugh." Humor can be the anesthesia for our unspoken pains.

In other growing pains, I am also learning that you cannot answer every call you get. That cuts into family time as well. Remember, it takes a village, but it helps the village when the lessons start in the hut. As Representative Maxine Waters says, "I'm reclaiming my time."

We should all reclaim our time and be mindful in protecting our energy. If you are in a good space and the person on the other end of that phone is calling to fill your ear with issues you can't do anything about, why keep answering? It's only going to frustrate you and make you mad. Don't get big mad. Protect your space by sifting out the negative energy.

It's as if we—especially men—have been programmed to let the smallest details divide our communities further. When I started my barbershop in the 1990s, there were a few guys in my area cutting hair. Most were cutting in their homes. When I got my license to start in business, I sought out area stylists for my shop so they could get certified as well.

We were in the middle of nowhere, in a field of dreams on a rural road running through a small town, but clients started coming from more than three counties away. When I asked them, "How did you find us way out here?" the answer was often "Word of mouth." That was a real compliment in the days before GPS.

Of course, the barbers in my shop frequently ended up wanting to open their own salons, and I always supported that because I'd wanted my own business too. We must support black businesses, even when they are not our own. I never tore other barbers down. That is counterproductive in establishing the economic sustainability we need in our communities.

Although, I've watched men pumping gas at a station and the owner changes the price of gas every day. Those men never say a mumbling word about the price changes of gas to the owner. However, if my price changes two dollars, once in twenty plus years, the same brothers will say, "Whew-wee that's too much! I can cut my own beard at home." In my Chris Rock voice, I say, "That ain't right!"

This psychological discomfort we have with spending with our own people is part of the theory of postulate 6. Postulate 6 is "Just say no to combative economics." But, before we get to postulate 6, we must first challenge a theory in postulate 5 about the customer always being right.

Postulate 5

A CUSTOMER IS NOT ALWAYS RIGHT

ARE CUSTOMERS REALLY, always right? Anytime you add the word *always* to a belief, there will almost *always* be examples in which that general rule is wrong. For instance, a guy with pink hair bought a ticket just to shoot up a movie theater; he killed twelve and injured seventy. Was he right just because he bought a movie ticket?

If simply going shopping is the key to being right, then there are thousands of people in malls right now who are never wrong, just for shopping.

Now, don't get me wrong. I get it: management created this cliché to avoid having an employee at a fast-food restaurant tell a customer, "I know you ordered a Big Mac with no pickles, but I put pickles on it because I think it tastes better that way." The cliché was created to avoid such incidents.

Yet we can't stifle all the logic, trying to idiot-proof our society. The customer is not always right. Customers are always wrong when they go to black-owned businesses looking for the hookup. Asking for discounts in black businesses is flawed.

Sill though, I've heard this a thousand times: "Brother man, how much are you going to charge me? Brother man, can you hook me up?" Since we are calling for reparations for the work our ancestors did years ago, we must be willing to pay for the work we see black folks doing for us here today!

It is up to us to make our communities whole, and we cannot do that if we are trying to shortchange each other. Our mindsets must seek out opportunities to circulate dollars back into our own communities.

If we do that, we will reinvent the Black Wall Streets once seen in the South. Now, we all know people who are doing good things to make our communities better. When we are fortunate enough to have those businesses, programs, and organizations serving to make things better for us, we cannot afford to shortchange those crucial entities.

If we can work hard to increase our vertical leaps to dunk a basketball, we cannot be shy about elevating our financial contributions to black owned businesses in our own communities.

A major obstacle is our mental conditioning; we are programmed to practice combative economics instead of collective economics.

For example, my salon has operated with a level of excellence for more than thirty years. Sadly, about 95 percent of my clients haven't tipped me a dime in over thirty years of faithful service. About 4 percent tip but not much more than a dime.

That leaves only 1 percent of my client base who really understand the importance of gratuity to black businesses. These statistics are specific to my own establishment, but I find that barbers and beauticians in our communities rarely get adequately compensated for their efforts in serving our own people.

Most of us wouldn't stiff servers at LongHorn Steakhouse, especially if the service was great. However, when it comes to our own color, we can sit in a black man's business for thirty years and not only short change on the tip but also have to be reminded to pay for the haircut.

Yet we say the customer is always right. The cliché sounds good, but just because you're a consumer, that alone is not enough to make you always right.

Economic restitution is essential for reconstructing our communities. Our reparations must start with a willingness to pay ourselves. Other communities invest in themselves by recirculating dollars spent within those respective communities. Studies show the average lifespan of a dollar is twenty-eight days in Asian communities, nineteen days in Jewish communities, and seventeen days in white communities. However, in our culture, a dollar leaves the black community in a matter of six hours, not days.

I know a brother with seemingly every pair of Nikes in existence. This brother has never been able to play a lick of ball, but he has a brand-new pair of Nikes' on his feet every week. Nike's costs get higher every time a black man wins an NBA championship. Yet this brother has never flinched at Nike's prices. But when I told him I had gone up on my price by five dollars in twenty years, the brother acted as if I were trying to pull his teeth!

Another day, a preacher came into my salon with the cleanest pair of alligator shoes I've ever seen. The reverend got out of his Cadillac Escalade, stepping so high that he looked as if he were trying to high jump over six dead bodies. That man of God was in a Versace suit with a Gucci belt, and he made sure to turn his jacket inside out so that we could all see how good God had been to him. The good reverend was as clean as a fish at the bottom of the ocean. He was shucking some corn, as we say in the South.

The preacher inhaled with an asthmatic rasp to his voice that all southerners know. The reverend came into our salon as if he were in the middle of his sermon from a church pulpit. I thought the minister was about to take us to the bridge when he kept saying, "God is good!"

I said, "All the time," as we are trained to do in our culture.

But when I informed the reverend that I had to go up on my prices by three dollars, he wiped his forehead clean with his handkerchief and shouted, "Good God Almighty! The devil is a lie."

Combative economics kills our communities. Alligator shoes ain't cheap. Escalades do nothing to elevate the economic conditions for us here in our town. Gucci made a mock blackface turtleneck sweater, which speaks volumes about Gucci's sensitivity to black people.

While at my black-owned business, I have provided economic opportunities for black folks no one else would hire—and those people in turn put their money into a collection plate for the preacher to buy those alligator shoes. It seems as if we are willing to go out of our way to support every entity except those created for us and by us (FUBU).

Harley-Davidson can sell a kickstand for $120. We don't have to know anything about William Harley or Arthur Davidson, but we will pay whatever they charge for a kickstand without blinking nor batting an eye.

Harley-Davidson released a Confederate edition motorcycle, yet we still purchase all their products, regardless of their cost. I wonder if I could sell a Confederate edition haircut for $120 in my community. It sounds like a good gimmick. Seeing that black folks don't mind paying for Gucci or even Harley Davidson even after the black disrespect. But, I would never disrespect my ancestry and the people I love like that. Plus, what good is it to gain the world and lose your soul?

Some of us come into a barbershop like Chris Rock's character in *I'm Gonna Git You Sucka* and say, "Thirty dollars for a haircut? Good Lawd! How much will it cost to let me just spin around in your barber's chair?"

When it is black businesses like ours that give money to kids in college who don't even graduate. Black businesses like ours sponsor football teams that don't win a game. Black businesses like ours sponsor beauty queens in pageants even when the beauty queens aren't even pretty. I'm sorry—I might have gone too far with that last one. But as Kirk Franklin said when he got upset, "for those of you that think that gospel music has gone too far," sometimes Negroes will make you want to stomp!

One of my clients didn't want to pay me five dollars to trim his beard. He actually asked me to lend him a pair of clippers so he could do the job himself at home. Do you still think the customer is always right?

On another note, if the customer is always right, on April 8, 2021, why was I denied access to Chimneys Golf Course in Winder, Georgia? On what would've been my Big Ma's 118th birthday, I went to join Chimneys Golf Course. I waited in line to get to the register. In the facility, two white men were buying balls, tees, and a round of golf.

When I got to the register, I asked to pay for a membership and a round of golf.

The registrar, Gary Cooper, told me, "The golf course is now owned by the City of Winder and we are not accepting new members, nor will you be able to play here until June."

I told Gary, "Thank you," even though I thought that sounded as strange as strange fruit; I had just witnessed two white men buy a round of golf right in front of me. Did Gary deny me access simply because I had a mask on?

As I walked back to my truck, I saw that the driving range was busy. I also noticed a long line of golf carts out, cleaned up, and patiently waiting for folks to come play. I even noticed a white child who looked to be no more than four years old driving a golf cart. The visual of that little kid's freedom from the golf course rules was a vision of a world that has never existed for people of color like me. My Big Mama, was born in 1903, and she certainly never felt the freedoms this white child was already experiencing in his four short years.

Every time I let my children, with driver's licenses, operate golf carts in our region, some country club employee would always ask my children for ID. White supremacy is a system that stops black youths and searches them for IDs, even on the deserted rural trails of backwoods golf courses! Yet we say the customer is always right.

In Winder, the customer is always right as long as the customer is always white. At Chimneys that day, I, a black customer, was right—outside.

After my experience, I emailed Winder's mayor, David Maynard. He spoke to me with an arrogance that only seeps through a white man's teeth. Our town must also take notice that David is the brother of the president of Maynard Realty. Since he has been mayor, Winder has been expanding like Putin's Soviet Union.

The City of Winder has been developed so much that a cow that used to live in a huge, lonely pasture is now stuck within a small fence beside a national chain store. I'll bet it's a milk cow in the little town of Bethlehem, trying to figure out why the City of Winder keeps on *moo*ving.

The entitlement of supremacy causes men to be delusional enough to believe black people should shut up and let them lecture us about our own experiences. We know when we have been discriminated against, although the mayor brushed it off as just poor customer service.

Finally, though, the mayor and the city did get around to a halfhearted apology—of course, only after the public pressure. The policy that the Mayor claimed limited new members must've only applied to me, because the golf course had just recently accepted eighteen new members, according to my open records request. Knowing all that, the mayor asked me, "Do you really think I should fire Gary?"

I told him Gary was not the only problem we have here. We need to correct the culture that keeps reproducing the Gary Coopers, David Maynards, and George Wallaces of the world. Then we will make our communities more inclusive as we sweep out our Chimneys.

Weeks later, Winder's administrator, Mandi Cody, emailed me an apology for my experience and offered me a free membership for just one year. I respectfully declined. Because, how would my playing golf free for one year keep the next person of color from being racially discriminated against by the toxic City of Winder?

What I proposed was a better resolution, for a lifetime membership with three guest passes per month. That way, I could take three kids from town who probably have never seen a golf course at all. That would expose the children to something different from what they saw all day and would give the staff at Chimneys an opportunity to see more diversity. Lord knows that staff needs the training.

I have not heard back from any city council member about my resolution. As Maya Angelou said, when people show you who they are, believe them. In 2022, it's a damn shame for a sitting city council to be mute about racial discrimination.

Some leaders will abandon their political powers given to them by black people who stood in long lines to support them as candidates.

Some supposed leaders will bend over backward just to wipe the dust off a white man's shoes.

This fictional world we have been duped into believing in doesn't really exist. God loves us too, and He is the designer of the entire universe. Therefore, we should put no man before God. Plus, what does it profit us to assimilate into a fictitious world and lose our real souls?

When something this egregious happens to any person, we must all choose a side. If you are on the side with the righteous, the righteous should know it. If you remain neutral, you have chosen the wrong side.

In the wake of the murder of our brother George Floyd, we must understand that we are in our intertestamental period; this is the time to join in righteous indignation. This is not a time for shrinking in the face of wrong just to wipe the dust off of a white man's shoes.

We must all wrestle within truth, regardless of race, nationality, or affiliation. Stand with what you know is right to show that you're standing against what you know is wrong. Silence is complicity. And as MLK said, "In the end, we will remember not the words of our enemies but the silence of our friends."

We still have too many self-preserving Negroes who are willing to sacrifice the greater good of the community for their own personal interests. In doing so, they give life and limb to try to assimilate into a world that has never really existed. The truth is, if there ever was a white man's world, your blackness would never be able to fit into it anyway. So be true to who you are, and keep it real!

We activists hurt more when we are betrayed by our own people, because we sacrifice so much of ourselves in taking stances for mistreated people. For instance, I have been up on the courthouse steps to protest another father's son being beaten in jail while my sons were safe at home.

Dedicated activists will be at school board meetings to protest other mothers' daughters' school suspensions while our own daughters are receiving awards. Most activists could live quiet, comfortable, self-serving lives if they chose to.

Yet activists sacrifice a lot without complaining, because we love our people. Which makes it sadder to see our own people join in solidarity with evil just to seclude us. Leaving activists alone on Activist Island is a common expectation in rural area codes. Betrayal of isolated activists is a reoccurring common theme too.

The absolute betrayal by your very own people is what really stings like a bee! It is also discouraging when you become the target of aggressions and microaggressions only to look around to find that the people you've helped are gone. I have been standing up for my living people just to look over my shoulder and feel only the presence of my dead ancestors standing with me. But as the song says, when you walk with Jesus, you'll never walk alone.

Although, it is easy to understand the frustrations if you put yourself in the activist's seat. The Dred Scott decision reincarnates itself, leaving some to think that a black man has no rights that a white man is bound to respect. This belief is emboldened in the South only because our sleeping soldiers won't rise up!

After I posted about my experience at the golf course, I had brothers calling and texting, wanting to be news reporters instead of news makers. Citizens who are willing to be news makers are more useful in these times.

News makers don't just say they are sorry for a wrong that happened to you or leave you hanging by saying, "We are praying for you." Praying is a great place to start. But praying cannot be the finish line. We must pray for God to guide our actionable steps to receive justice in this world. And when God orders our steps, we must be faithfully courageous in taking them!

More encouraging to me was the response I got from a white woman; she sent a complaint to the mayor's office and to the golf course. Allies don't just have your back; allies are willing to walk up front for and with you.

Fannie Lou Hamer said, "We can pray until we faint, but unless we get up and try to do something about it, God is not going to put it in your lap."

Political power emerges from people taking personal responsibility to help others. Also, as my cousin J.W. says, "We must watch as well as pray." It speaks volumes when we see a rainbow coalition coming together in common causes for justice. One white ally said to me that she was uptown ready to kick some ass on my behalf.

I told her she needed to come on back from up yonder! I made it clear that I wasn't trying to cause another insurrection, as Trump did. Although I will say, similar to Trump, "White allies like that are some very fine people, and we love you." All I ask is that you don't put on no Viking hat for me.

Postulate 6

JUST SAY NO TO COMBATIVE ECONOMICS

IN SOLVING PROBLEMS within our communities, it is crucial for us to first identify the major obstructions holding us back. In my experience as a business owner and as the son of an entrepreneur, it is clear to me that combative economics is one of our top public enemies.

To put combative economics into simple plain southern words, we are programmed to stay at odds with each other over finances. Hence, we have a culture built on combat and confrontation. Now, since I've been exposed to this mental programming myself, I already know what you might be thinking: *The reason I don't spend my money with black businesses is because black folks don't ever do right.*

Is that really true, or is it just what we are programmed to believe? If we are really being honest, some of us think that by our black-on-black birthright, we really expect a whole lot from our businesses without paying anything.

From the years I have spent in observation of my rural community, I can conclusively say that too many of us want you to do a whole lot of something for next to, or absolutely nothing. In the new English urban translation, we come in looking for the hook up! Holler if you hear me?

It is easy to detect the leaches around a beauty salon because they are always coming into your establishment making sure that you see them reaching for a broom. But after their hair is slayed you won't see them reaching for their wallets. "Oh, my purse was in the car." Well, if you can find my broom to show me, show me the money I have earned for your service. This is a hair salon, sweeping only pays the bills if you are the janitor.

From the time I started working with my father at five years old, I also noticed that there would be excessive expectations from people who looked like us. On a daily basis I heard things like "Can I pay you Tuesday for the work I want done today?"

Also, as a man in the service industry, who has run one of the few completely black-owned businesses in my community for more than thirty-six years, as I said before, I've had 99 problems, but a tip ain't one.

Even in witnessing customers' tendencies in my father's business and in my own, I too am not immune to my own negative thinking, as it pertains to how I can falsely perceive my own people.

Therefore, I have realized that if I want to fix the state of the system, first I have to fix me.

The counselor I had in college told me a story of how two businesses can sell the same thing, but we are conditioned to believe that the products from white owners are inherently better.

Back in the day, before refrigerators were common, people had ice boxes to keep their perishable foods cold. You would have to buy a big block of ice, to put into your freezer, to help keep your food from spoiling. A white man across town had a huge ice freezer, to make blocks of ice, to sell to the public. Let's say for conversational purposes, the man's name was Vanilla Ice.

Vanilla Ice used horse and buggy to transport his blocks of ice all over town. As you can guess, he served the suburban communities near his freezer first, early in the morning while it was still cool. The blocks were huge on Vanilla's side of town, but they were melted down to ice cubes by the time he reached the ghettos. And of course, Vanilla Ice sold ice cubes to black folks for a much higher price than he had sold ice blocks to whites. Talk about a need for a contract with black America!

Anyway, the blacks lived in much poorer communities. So, it was a struggle to scrape up enough money to buy from Vanilla Ice. But they did what they had to, to keep Vanilla happy because, southern rule number one states, "Never piss a white man off." Blacks were forced by means of terrorism to either buy white in the daytime or expect to see white sheets at night.

In the meantime, a wise John Henry–like Negro observed Vanilla's operation. John Henry knew firsthand the community's issues, because he lived there. He knew the community needed more than just a few leftover ice cubes. He also understood that impoverished people would not be able to continuously afford Vanilla Ice's hiked-up prices.

John Henry saved up enough money to purchase a huge ice freezer, and set it up only to sell in his community. Henry understood well southern rule number one, in that he'd better not be caught trying to sell his ice on the white side of town. He would push his cart of ice blocks door-to-door first thing in the morning; he could also deliver virtually on demand for a third of what Vanilla Ice was charging, because John had compassion for his people.

First thing every morning, John Henry's blocks of ice were so huge that a single block would not fit into most black people's iceboxes. So, he would use a sledgehammer to custom shape the ice blocks, to make the blocks perfectly fit into his customers' freezers.

Observers admired John Henry's skillfulness with the sledgehammer so much that they gave him the nickname Hammer. People would ask him, "Hammer, how do you do it?"

Hammer humbly shrugged and said, "I don't know. I guess I got it like that."

Everyone in the community was happy. They could afford Hammer's prices, and he even extended credit to those in need. Hammer also gave the leftover shavings from his ice to his neighbors to put in their iced tea.

Hammer was doing okay, until Vanilla Ice noticed his sales were down. Vanilla asked around and found out from Deacon Willy (nicknamed the watchman) that Hammer was also in the ice business. That night, Deacon Willy and Vanilla Ice both terrorized the town.

The next morning, Hammer strolled through the village several times without being able to give away one single block of ice for free. Puzzled, Hammer asked Willy the watchman, "Deacon Willy, why doesn't anybody want to take a free block of ice from me?"

Deacon Willy, who usually saw everything, replied, "I ain't seen nothing! It might be because that white man's ice is way colder than yours."

The conclusion that a white man's ice is somehow colder is not the strangest thing I've ever seen black folks believe. Although in similar conditions, water freezes at exactly the same temperature!

Being white does not make someone inherently racist, nor does it make a person genetically better. There was a time when black people were thought to be inferior in athletics. Sports were deemed too challenging for Negroes. Looking at the careers of Floyd Mayweather Jr., Jim Brown, and LeBron James, we see how absurd that idea was.

Researching that mindset further, we discover that many of our scientific advancements were the works of people of color too. We've had to work twice as hard to get a fraction of the credit, and we've only ended up getting one half of the one percentage of the economic restitution that we are due! Talk about the need for a contract with black America!

On the black hand side though, it is downright embarrassing the hostile way we can engage each other when it comes to the almighty dollar. The O'Jays sang, "For the love of money, people will steal from their mother and rob from their own brothers". Might I add, some of us will sneak stuff out of our sisters' purses too. For decades, the infectious disease of combative economics has been hitting our communities way harder than the coronavirus ever could.

Scenes from Ice Cube's movie *Barbershop* really do happen. A client jumped out of my chair and ran out of my barbershop without paying for his service. I went to the door and yelled, "Hey man! When are you going to pay me for your haircut?"

He yelled back, "When the Waffle House closes."

I have a feeling that I might not ever get paid, because the Waffle House is open 24 hours a day and seven days a week. The Waffle House was still open during the pandemic and even on Christmas Eve. Black man to black man, I guess that brother was wishing my black-owned business a merry combative Christmas.

A small piece of paper carries a lot of weight. And in my rural town, even the coins are very heavy too.

Once I purchased a vending machine, so our clients could have something to snack on as they waited. I would buy Snickers bars at Sam's Club for sixty-eight cents each and sell them for seventy-five cents; my seven-cent profit per bar would never pay off the $3,000 cost of the vending machine. Seven cents of profit aren't nearly enough in compensation to pay myself back for stocking the machine, nor any of the other associated expenses.

But, I wasn't thinking much about the profit margin when I invested in the machine. I was mostly considering the people who might get hungry while waiting to be served. Despite my being considerate and losing money while trying to help, I still had customers falsely claim that the manual machine stole their money.

If you are not familiar with manual vending machines, it is almost impossible for those machines to take a person's money, without leaving the proof of the money or the evidence of the product stuck in the machine.

The more I think about it, the more I realize I was committing black-on-black crime against myself, by not charging enough and by letting clients con me out of three quarters. I've always been a better person than a businessman.

I've had a bad habit of putting the wants and needs of the people I love before my own. What I have learned from those experiences is that people will treat you as badly as you let them. These self-inflicted wounds from combative economics taught me some valuable lessons. The old man in the barbershop once said, "a bought lesson is better than a taught lesson."

It was Tupac that said in "Changes," "That's just the way it is." Although in the original piece, Bruce Hornsby sang, "That's the way it is, but don't you believe them." While the serenity prayer teaches us to accept the things we cannot change.

However, the enlightened sister Angela Davis said it is up to us to change the things we can no longer accept. It is the optimistic approach we must use as our guide as we gravitate our nation away from its injustices. Hornsby's song, "The Way It Is," was about the civil rights struggle. Hornsby abandoned his white male privilege, to change the things he could no longer accept. He did this by utilizing his God given talents as a tool for expression in embracing the righteous side of our culture.

It might help us to recruit more white allies to the right side if we recognized the righteous, and stopped accepting the glorification of the sinister on the sides of mountains.

If John Brown's face was carved on the side of Stone Mountain, I would by all of my family season passes and take children from all over the community there every week. John Brown was a white man who had all of the blessings that America promised, yet he valiantly chose to die and sacrificed his sons' lives for the Negro cause too.

Viola Liuzzo abandoned her white northern privilege to come south to drive marchers and protestors back to Selma from Montgomery. On March 25, 1965 on the rural Route 80 in Alabama, Viola was ambushed and killed by four KKK members. One of those four Klansman was found out to also be an FBI agent.

Therefore, we should no longer accept J. Edgar Hoover's name hoisted up on any building with pride. And we should honor the righteous side of white history to teach our children to do what is right!

Why aren't these narratives taught in our schools? The answer, my friend, is blowing in the wind. These answers are blowing in the wind and The Southern Awakening is a method of seeing these answers, as we let the wind elevate our gaze to the sky. Embracing this paradigm shift is the key to your awakening!

As you arrive, you will see the blackbirds flying high through the air collectively together. You will also notice that the birds are navigating the skies in a triangular form almost perfectly designed in the shape of an arrow. One blackbird will fly in the front to make it aerodynamically easier for the followers to glide in its trail. When that lead bird grows weary, another one emerges, assuming the front position. They all fly together as a team—a strategy we should use here on the ground.

We are meant to fly high and maintain an elevated perspective. We were not designed to be crabs, nor in a bucket! From your elevated plane, it is plain to see these crabs must be rescued out of these confining buckets, and properly placed back into their natural habitats of the unending seas. We are enamored in our rightful positions. For it is in our proper context that we will obtain this glorious power! We could support one another better if we weren't down on the ground, scrambling and scrapping over three measly quarters.

One of my clients lived in a rusty trailer home. Now, there's nothing wrong with living wherever you can afford. But this client complained about the price of my candy bars, saying, "Seventy-five cents? Shoot, I am not going to be making the barber rich."

Now, this client who believed his spending seventy-five cents could make me rich was living right next door to his mother's rusty house trailer, which was only inches away from his grandfather's rusty house trailer. Just the visual of 3 homes wedged that extremely close together would make my uncle Herman say, "Now that's a hazard!"

Anyway, I told the brother that one of those three quarters must be the one Michael Jackson pitched into the homeless man's cup in the "Billie Jean" video. "You might want to keep that magical three quarters you got from David Blaine and Copperfield, and carefully place all three in an armored truck to take them back home with you.

There are three generations of rust and poverty you should pitch those three quarters at back home before you come over here and magically make this barber rich." Oprah Winfrey can say your name and make you rich. Tyler Perry can make a lot of us rich. Jay-Z and Beyoncé are Mansa Musa reincarnated, helping black people build wealth all across the globe. Three quarters is not enough to make a kid in a candy store smile, much less be enough to make a grown man rich.

Our mindsets are combative in nature because we operate as if we are at odds with one another for no reason. Why can't we just like both Jay-Z and Nas?

People, it is ok to think that both Tupac and Biggie were great lyricists! We are the only culture who will pit one brother against another, when it makes absolutely no sense. Black folks had an all-out culture war pitting Michael Jackson against Prince, when it's obvious that a black man in high-water pants and another in high-heeled shoes don't have any business beefing with each other!

LeBron James is the dominant basketball player in this era, just as Michael Jordan was in his time. It should be that simple. Meantime, I've never seen one argument in the barbershop almost break out into a fistfight over whether Larry Bird was better than Jerry West. I've never seen other cultures try to diminish the accomplishments of Bart Starr or Joe Namath just to build Tom Brady up. We are too consumed with combat in our communities

As if that's not bad enough, I once watched a woman, who could barely pick up her feet, slide right by my vending machine, looking all mean, and then go two miles to a convenience store to buy the same Snickers bar for two dollars.

Combative economics makes people say and do silly things, such as "We're going over there and giving the barber our money." If you think you're *giving* your barber or hairstylist money for nothing, the value you place on his or her time and talent is zero.

How many times have you seen a magical parade of people walk into a salon, hand money to the barber or beautician, and then just turn around and leave without getting a service done? If you get a haircut from me, you paid me for that. If you were provided great service and you skipped on the tip, you have slighted a black business for its service.

I had a client with jet black and ashy feet, who would come into the barbershop wearing sandals because he'd just gotten a pedicure. The ashy feet brother would come into our business bragging about how much he tipped those Asian ladies for his foot service, when it was obvious that he wasn't tipping them enough for them to put some lotion on his black and ashy feet!

This less aware brother was also making a joke about not knowing what those Asian ladies were saying, during his foot service. Meanwhile, he could understand every single word that was coming out of my mouth, but he had never thought to tip my black owned business a dime! You should tip outside your culture as long as you're tipping inside your culture as well. Do you know what I'm saying?

Our economic plan for our community has to start on a basis of personal responsibility. If we show love to other cultures, then it is about time we start showing some love to ourselves. I wish we had as many people invested in supporting black businesses as we have to approach us to support their charitable ideas.

One woman came to my salon because she had seen a kid uptown whose hair, she thought, looked bad. Mind you, this lady was not even my client, but my business is the first one she thought of when she had an idea for a charity.

And of course, the concept of helping someone out sounds good on the surface. But who was the only person making a sacrifice in that scenario? The lone barber of course, because I was the one providing a service for free.

But this lady who had only saw a nappy headed kid and brought him to me was running around town bragging about how she got the kid a free haircut.

Then, of course, the woman came back to the barbershop with six other sad stories about how these nappy headed kids were in need. But my momma didn't raise no educated fool.

So, I politely suggested to the woman, being that this was her charitable cause, how about we make a fairer deal. I suggested that she only pay half price for each hair cut to help remove half of the load of burden from the barber, for her charitable cause.

I thought that seemed reasonable since it was her heart's calling. Right? After I proposed that she pay half, I guess all the nappy-headed kids in our community disappeared, or they all caught the mange because she never saw any more nappy heads that she thought needed a haircut! As Snoop Dogg said, "Everybody got their cup, but they ain't chipped in."

There are people in our community who sit in the back of the church, wanting to be the boss of the choir, musicians, deacons, and the pastor too. They talk big but they haven't contributed five dollars to the church in five years! But the moment they get sick or behind on their house payments, they come begging for the church to save them. And when I say *save them*, I don't mean their souls. They couldn't care less about their souls. All they seek is the almighty dollar.

Three guys from our community once formed an organization called Young Men Chasing Dreams. It sounded great, but none of the founders had a job at the time. If they were trying to guide youth in a right direction, at least one of them needed to know which way to go.

As the town's barber, I listened to their spectacular ideas, and I waited with anticipation to hear the plan for how we were going to pay for all these great ideas. The plan for finances was the, go-to, move we always use in our community. One guy said, "We can sell some plates"!

The man said it like he was mentioning a new economic plan that we have never heard before. If you are from the country, I know you've heard that plan of "selling plates" to generate money before? We have to evolve past the idea of thinking that our churches can sustain themselves by selling plates. Established restaurants are losing money trying to sell food. I rode past a Denny's and a Golden Corral, and they both look beat up and broken down from trying to sell plates.

Therefore, selling plates cannot be our primary source for fundraising. Heck, you probably can think of churches that have been selling plates for building funds for tens of years, and we have not seen a groundbreaking on the first building yet. We have been selling plates down here so long we should be worshiping in the Twin Towers of the South!

Regardless, the Young Men Chasing Dreams mentor said we could sell plates to raise money. I asked them who would buy the plates and the food that would go on them, and one said, "We could ask your mama to bake us one of her famous pound cakes."

I replied, "Young man, my mother is on a fixed income. Unless you have the money to pay her for her time and her costs, you might as well change the name of this organization from Young Men Chasing Dreams to Grown Men Chasing Cakes!"

Our elderly has already sacrificed enough for us in their lifetimes. As kings, we should come up with ways to take care of them. They have done their part for us to be here in the first place, and we need not burden them with our ideas. As kings, we must lift our elderly up to show them we have learned from their examples.

Quarantining during the COVID-19 pandemic has afforded all of us some dear time to reflect on our lives. In the movie *American Skin*, Nate Parker's character is a father, who had to watch helplessly as his fourteen-year-old son was killed by the police.

Parker is also a military veteran, trained to die for his country, yet he is asked to stand at ease to allow the murderer of his only son, walk away scot-free. Parker suffers enormous grief. He is extremely frustrated, having been unable to protect his only son. If you are a parent, I hope you can understand a righteous rage about your kid? Nat Turner's rebellion was also caused because people were full of righteous indignation.

When I see men protecting their children, I often think about my dad. I remember the day I came home from kindergarten crying because a much older bully, named Paul, beat me up and took my *Starsky and Hutch* Hot Wheels car.

I told my father what happened when he got home from work, and he immediately put me in the front seat of the car. My dad threw his shot gun in the back seat, and we rode right over to the bully's parents' house. The much older bullies' parents and my dad had a real nice and cordial conversation about the ordeal. Thankfully, Paul's parents were extremely remorseful about what he had done to me. They assured my dad that nothing like this would ever happen again.

Satisfied that it wouldn't, my dad drove off, and about a quarter mile up the dirt road from Paul's house. My dad then casually reached in the back seat, grabbed his shot gun, and with one hand fired off the shells into the night sky. The booming sound of that rifle ricocheted in my thoughts all through the night.

As a little child I didn't have the words to understand what any of that meant. At that young age the only thing I wanted to say was "hey what about my Starsky and Hutch Hot Wheels car? Although there wasn't a single word verbalized between us, I completely understood that my father would always be there ready to protect me, no matter what!

On November 19, 1985, my mom asked me nicely about four times, to get up out of bed and get ready for school. I heard her each time, but I rolled over and pulled the covers back over my head. It was as if I was still wanting her to dig me out from under the covers like she did when I was a little boy. But then, my father casually walked by my bedroom and nonchalantly mumbled, "Get up boy." I jumped up got dressed and was at attention before his shadow got past my bedroom door.

After that, I was on my way to catch the school bus, when Johnny Frank, who worked for my dad, came running up to our house yelling, "Roscoe done got killed out here!"

My dad was grading our front yard, when the seat broke on the bulldozer he was riding. He fell to the earth right in the path of the moving bulldozer. My father, my rock, and the protective shield I admired immensely was crushed, in to this cold and bitter earth.

My mother ran out of the house to try to rescue the only man she had ever loved. But it was obvious in the instant, even his most devoted help mate could not help him now. My distraught mother lingered lifelessly at the side of my father's broken up, bloody bruised and battered corpse.

Through my glaring lens of gray, I saw a mirage of my mother molding in to this cold and bitter earth, to be with my dad. I stood there crippled, paralyzed by the panic. Somehow, I knew if I didn't move, I would be stuck there frozen, watching both of my parents' lights fade to gray. It was then that my mama's-boy instincts rushed me out to the scene to try to dig out some of the fragments of the family that I had left.

As I moved closer to the site, my mom's gaze shifted from my dad to me. Her gloomy glare glanced back at me with the sparkle of life that just a moment ago I believed was gone for good too. Although devastated by the death that had done her part, my queen mother chose to vacate my father's side, as a sacrifice, to save the soulless gray spirit of her youngest son.

"Stop! Don't come any closer!" she said. "Your daddy wouldn't want you to see him like this!" My mom got up and grabbed me quickly while covering my eyes to spare me from what she'd seen. Mama bears are always trying to protect their cubs, but my mama didn't know that her baby cub had already seen too much.

I realize now that culturally, we need to remove the stigma we have put on counseling. I could have used some professional help after seeing all that I saw. Although life did teach me some very valuable lessons in the waning moments when the buzzards started hovering over my father's dead body. Those damn buzzards started circling around my dad's blood- and sweat-drenched corpse before it was even cold.

The worst part about it was that the buzzards wasn't the birds circling us in the air. The cruelest buzzards surrounding us were on the ground. A few of my father's relatives felt that my mother should get out of her own house that she and her husband had shared, together. Here I was struggling to fill this huge sunken hole in my heart and these vultures who knew we were without my dad, wanted us to also be without our own home.

The buzzards in the sky aren't as merciless as the ones on the ground. Buzzards from the sky will at least wait until something is deceased before they pick and pluck from the dead's bodies. These ruthless vultures on the ground will try to pick and pluck from a breathing widow who is still grieving and trying to take care of her living kids.

Dinah Washington sang, "If my life is like the dust that hides the glow of a rose, what good am I?"

While processing the enormity of hurt and devastation, I instantly became the man of the house. It was too much for me at first. I acted out negatively, not having the words or the tools to process a world that seemed as new as the day I was born. Most of the advice I got was "Just pray about it. We're praying for you." I love prayer, and I did appreciate that. I do understand people's good intentions.

However, I was devastatingly grief-stricken in this world without my protective covering. Without my dad I felt as naked as a newborn.

We have to remove the stigma we have on counseling in our culture. I know I could've used a toolbox with some tools in it, in addition to those prayers. A professional's help can give you some useful tools to guide you through the process of grief.

Those tools are definitely needed because our society has some intrusive people who will invade your space at the worst times. They are like news reporters who only want to get the story before they even know if you are all right. The nosey and inconsiderate people, who will just pop up at your house unexpectedly, are usually the same ones who are fascinated with reality TV.

I was only fourteen at the time of my dad's death. The moment my father died, I was treated like a professional athlete who had just lost a basketball game. It didn't take long for a rush of press rows flashing lights to bombard me with thousands of invasive and insensitive questions: "What happened? What did you see? What time was it? What are you guys going to do with your dad's tractor?"

Concern and sympathy are not the same as compassion and empathy. Even the best intentions meant with love are not always the most helpful in a crisis.

We need to give people the time they need to process traumatic events. No one should expect a child to want to live such a devastating event once, much less have to relive it a thousand times on the first day. Excessive questioning is cruelly insensitive, especially in dealing with children. If and when someone wants to talk to you about something, you'll know it. You won't have to ask.

From that, I learned how to allow suffering people the space they need to heal. I learned that I can pray for you without even letting you know it. I can also leave a card in your mailbox, to let you know I'm here, while allowing you the space you'll need to heal. Understandably, some of those well-intentioned people were identifying and trying to process their own personal pains through our struggle.

But the proper place for your grief is not putting that burden on another person who is already grieving. That is why we should all seek some professional help.

My family went through some difficult times after my father's death. Our weeping endured way more than a many of nights. However, joy comes cascading in the moments when I realize how blessed I was to have worked for my dad in the summers.

Having seen my father interact with people outside the home benefits me until this very day; he taught me the importance of treating people fairly in business and in life in general. Dad also taught me about collective economics in the way he helped others start their own businesses too.

The joy I found to help me discover some happy days came to me through the therapy of the creative energy exercised in becoming Barnard the Barber. Because we have this stigma in our community about getting professional counseling, some of us utilize our barbers as our non-paid therapeutic sessions.

As a professional, I know that no one goes to a barbershop to hear the barber's problems. Therefore, all I am asking you to consider is that while you are laying down your burdens on your barber, your barber may be bottling up a bath tub full of internal struggles of his very own?

Seeing my father crushed, into this cold and bitter earth, is tough to think about even now. But if it takes me opening up to share my story, to help guide you to your path in freeing yourself from your grief and your pain, then this bitter earth may not be so bitter, after all. Those we love will never leave us; we can see them in the eyes of a child.

My father's light in life still teaches me so much, still at this very moment. His nickname was Dust, you see? Dust is floating around us everywhere, all the time. For it is the mighty yet easy southern winds who guide the dust to surround and comfort each of us every single day, and every day, like the dust, still I rise. And so will you!

Still to this very day, I will meet people who knew my father decades ago and they are overwhelmingly kind to me simply because of something he did for them many moons ago. Generational blessings I have done nothing to earn come to grace me at gates where my name is unknown. In our journeys, we too can plant seeds of goodness that our own seeds will harvest in generations to come.

The song "Optimistic" by Sounds of Blackness teaches us to keep our heads to the sky. Blackbirds know it's easier to soar in the sky collectively, and it is easier for us to come together in unison, on the ground, when we seek our guidance from the sky.

Postulate 7

PRIORITIZE COLLECTIVE ECONOMICS AS A FORM OF SELF-REPARATIONS

TO ALL THE allies who bought this book, congratulations! You have just passed the first negro standardized test for the day. Making it your personal responsibility to invest in entrepreneurs of color can be a way to personally exercise reparations, and when it comes to sustaining black-owned businesses, all money matters!

This theory encourages good folks from every walk of life to chip in. Heck, I don't mind if this book is required reading at a Ku Klux Klan book rally; read it! As long as you are not having the club meeting in front of my house, by all means, burn a cross or two!

Seriously though, we need to learn from one another to grow as a united community. When we talk about reparations, we normally discuss the issue from the standpoint of a public policy. Though such a public policy is necessary and long overdue, politics in America is extremely messy. Not to mention the garbage trucks full of tons of red tape. In the meantime, while we wait for this government to show some accountability, we can all make reparations our own personal responsibility right here and now today.

Each of us can intentionally seek out one new or a different black owned business to support at least once a month. If you are counting, that's only twelve black owned businesses to support per a year.

Which is a small sacrifice to make, for those people whose ancestors provided so much to our nation, and those debts have never been paid. Especially since all of my white neighboring churches love to point out how they went on a mission trip to Haiti or Africa. My thing is, hell you can save some of those traveling expenses, flying on Spirit Airlines, if you were willing to help some black folks out right here!

Another useful solution we can use is to apply what I call the one-third postulate: with a mindful intent, we can target and tip black workers and businesses at least one-third of the cost of their services.

That's a form of self-reparations. We all know the negative effects of disproportionate policing, prison sentencing, job discrimination, and voting restrictions. America has been blatantly intentional in messing things up for black folks. We need to be just as intentional in lifting our communities up. The one-third postulate for support is just a place to start. Eventually, by investing in our economic sustainability, we can reclaim some political power in the rural South.

The solution is for us to be as intentional in solving problems as some are in causing them. As Bob Marley asked, "If the people who are trying to make the world worse aren't taking a day off, how can I?"

Those are just two simple steps you can take today, by making it your personal responsibility, as a patriotic American, to help to repay a debt we all know that this great nation still owes. We need to clean up our side of the street so we can all peacefully walk down the road together. Dr. King said we must learn to live together as brothers or perish together as fools. That calls for a lot of tough conversations to begin at home. Another old southern saying is "You need to sweep your own yard first before you go sweeping up anybody else's."

The pandemic has granted us time to reflect on the simple things we were missing, that were of major importance. The most valuable time, and people, in our lives are usually at our homes. Have you ever met a parent who said, "Man, I wish I had spent less time at home with my children when they were growing up"? I have never heard any parent say that, although I have heard many parents say they regret not prioritizing more time at home with their families.

At one time, I was running my business, teaching chess at the Boys and Girls Club, fielding almost all the complaints as vice president of the local NAACP, and serving as the vice president of our elementary school's PTA as the lone black man there. Every time a brown kid needed a mentor, all the women in the PTA thought I should be it. I try with a good heart to do everything I can to serve others, but one day I found myself rolling up and down the school halls, going from kid to kid, and bouncing like a pinball off of the classroom doors.

The principal admired my efforts, especially since he'd also seen me coaching the baseball team. He said to me, "Barnard, you're always so busy around town. Don't you have children of your own? I know you mean well, but I think you're spreading yourself too thin. Being a mentor is a full-time commitment, and the last thing neglected children need is for one more person to let them down. The best way you can serve the mentoring program is to first make sure your own children don't need a mentor too."

I thanked the principal for his wisdom, and I started sweeping up my own backyard. Villages can become too dependent on one person with a willing heart. It takes teams of tribes to keep our villages running smoothly.

People also need to be more mindful in respecting parents' time that we set aside for our families as well. I was outside talking to my daughter one day, and an invasive neighbor intruded on our conversation to ask me a medical question. Barbers shouldn't have to be therapist nor twenty-four-hour orthopedic surgeons, but that didn't stop him from interrupting me, talking to my child, to ask us if he should have surgery on his knee.

I usually don't give medical advice, but it would have been unethical and irresponsible to not guide this black man with some advice in this situation. Therefore, I told this brother that I strongly believed that he should not have surgery on his knee.

The inquisitive brother then asked me, "why not?" I made him aware that since he had just sought a second opinion about his knee from a barber, and that there was no telling whom he would ask to perform the surgery next. In my medical opinion, I was a bit concerned that this brother might invasively ask a lumberjack, in the middle of him chopping down a tree, to do the surgery on his knee! It is wise to only take advice from the right sources at the proper time.

There are several other barbershops in my community, and we communicate frequently because some clients try to pit us against each other. My cousin owns a barbershop in town and charges thirty dollars for a haircut, which is the minimum for what all the other barbers should.

Dave, one of my clients, always came to me with a sad story, and I would sometimes cut his hair for ten dollars. But when our salon was closed due to the pandemic, I wasn't about to risk my life or my license by cutting hair on a discount. Dave kept texting me, "Man, your cousin charges thirty dollars. You're my barber. When are you going to open back up again my brother?"

I texted back the same message I had on my answering machine: "Sorry, but we are closed until the state-mandated shutdown is lifted due to COVID-19."

He replied, "Fear not. Feed your faith, and starve your doubt," in an attempt to manipulate the Word.

After that, I told Dave I would have to charge him the same thirty dollars, that all the other barbers charged, and I haven't heard a word from old slick Dave since. When I saw my friend Dave, I reminded him that in the Word, Judas betrayed Jesus over thirty coins too.

For me, the pandemic downtime was needed to plot a plan to focus on reconstructing my life to make some vertical changes. A vertical change involves doing something new and different from your primary source of income.

That doesn't mean you have to quit your job. It just means doing something outside your norm, or better yet, something you've always wanted to do. For example, a vertical change for me is acting, investing in real estate, and writing this book. A lateral move would be for me to open two more barbershops.

Vertical and lateral growth both can open opportunities for you to expand. However, it is vertical growth that opens up pathways to diversifying your revenue streams. Say for instance, if I had seven other hair salons, and one salon had to close because of COVID-19. Then all of my salons would have had to close too, because it was a statewide COVID restriction.

It's the same with anyone who owns multiple dry cleaners, car washes, or restaurants—all lateral moves. Any move that results in growth is still a good move. Although lateral moves may mean one obstruction might block your only path.

In chess, some pieces can be stuck or trapped because of how they can or can't move, but grand masters control their own destinies by contemplating possibilities most cannot envision. Open up your mind for some creative thinking, and believe in your ability to find a way.

Be the knight on a chessboard, a piece that can jump over other pieces, and it expands your ability to move vertically. You'll be amazed at what God can do through you. You can indeed become better than Bobby Fischer, Boris Spassky, and Magnus Carlsen combined. Chess is a metaphor for life, and as long as you believe in yourself, you're winning!

When I taught chess at the Boys and Girls Club, our mantra before each class was "I am smart! I am gifted! My next move will be my best move!" Say that while believing in your own abilities to create the opportunities your community needs.

In the movie *One Night in Miami*, directed by the multitalented and extra lovely sister Regina King, Sam Cooke's character says, "I don't want just a seat at the table. I want the recipe!" We have always had the recipe in us; we just keep allowing others to steal the credit for what we've cooked.

Vertical moves open up the flood gates for cultural changes. As you strive to make those vertical changes, prepare yourself to face forces that want to keep you stuck where they think you belong. Those forces may even be the people you've selflessly helped and love. But those forces don't actually have the power. The real power comes from within. The great sifter will reveal those forces for what they are, and cream will always rise to the top. As you grow, gravitate toward the forces that are trying to lift you up.

In prioritizing collective economics as a form of self-reparations, we must shift our mindsets from one-lane thinking. Everyone is not supposed to be on the same road.

From the day you are born, you are taught to go to college, in the hope that some company will give you a good-paying job. You then hope the company will stay in business for thirty years so you can retire. Then at your retirement party, the company may gift you a Citizen watch and a plaque with your name spelled wrong on it, and you will live happily ever after—that is, you will live off your pension for a few years until you die. That sounds really exciting, right? You're really dying the entire time unless you're doing what you love to do.

There is always some educated fool working in a cubicle who thinks he's a CEO. A brother once told me with his nose stuck up in the air, "Step into my office."

I said, "Bro, I can step over into your low-partitioned space." It is strange to see people with degrees sitting in a cubicle, convinced that they are somehow breathing different air from everyone else in the same plant.

This brother once told me, "You know, LeBron James should've gone to college like me. A mind is a terrible thing to waste."

I told this brother that I thought he was doing well and that I was happy he was so proud of what he'd achieved. However, his cubicle's height was no match for LeBron James's vertical leap. In fact, LeBron had just purchased an entire school full of cubicles, for his underserved community by following his life's divine path. We all have a path of our own that is uniquely given to us by our Creator. When we listen to God, he will guide us to our path.

If my son had an opportunity to make LeBron James's money, I would've taken my hand, that is made strong by the Almighty, and snatched his ass out of his cubicle in the third grade! I know that sounds extreme, but I am promising you that I would.

You go to college to get a good job to make more money, right? Therefore, if you capitalize on an opportunity to make more money, in one year than you could in thirty years sitting in somebody else's cubicle, while doing something you love, then you have just successfully made a vertical leap over an MBA and an educated fool at the same time.

Humor is just a good way to get a point across. And laughter is always a great way to anesthetize the trauma of the truth. Kevin Hart told us to laugh at his pain because it is therapeutic. The therapy of laughter makes you feel too good to feel bad.

I found my calm amidst the chaos by following motivational coach Celest Divine Ngeve on Instagram and Facebook. One day Celest said, "If you go through this pandemic and you come out on the other side of this the same, then you have successfully wasted all this good time. Challenge yourself to be better. Write that book!"

Celest's message reached me at a moment when I was—as most of us were—stuck at home in quarantine, just watching the ceiling fan go around. Her words resonated with my spirit, and I put pen to paper. This book is a vertical step in the climb to accomplish my dream of becoming a published author. Thank you Celest Divine Ngeve, for always selflessly giving your light, that shines as inspirational motivation, on a wretch like me!

Postulate 8

CHANGE YOUR POLITICAL LANDSCAPE, AND WE'RE MOVING ON UP!

THE SOUTHERN AWAKENING is a black man's guide to liberating the rural South, but realistically, we will need all hands-on deck to make the societal adjustments our nation needs. Being that I am a black man, I wrote this manifesto from my own personal perspective.

By now, I hope it's clear to every single person reading this book that you are the most critical and necessary component required for our awakening to manifest itself in the flesh! So, speak your mind. And by all means, use any media necessary. In this present age, platforms are not only accessible, He has placed the whole world in your hands. Just use them wisely and for righteous causes. Envision a world where every community has access to resources to achieve the American dream.

Through research, you'll find that self-sustainable communities are not new concepts. We will need to, with a righteous intent, exercise in collective economics to make it work. Your voice may very well be the nudge our society needs to be on the right side of history. Therefore, don't ever give up on humanity, because the harvest is plenty!

We already have established networks if we utilize the global platforms of the hair-care industry. We courageously speak our minds in our hair salons and our barbershops, right? Now, let's take that same energy to the streets! Also, we must prioritize circulating our dollars within our own communities, and do better in the way we patronize black owned businesses. It is up to us to emphasize personal responsibility as a form of self-reparations.

Solutions can be multifaceted. It's key that we must take personal responsibility first; however, without a plan for political solutions, the doors of opportunity will continue to slam in the faces of marginalized communities.

For instance, for years, I have used my barbershop to register eligible citizens to vote. But when Brian Kemp was secretary of state in 2016–2017, Georgia kicked out more than half a million registered voters from the registration roll. Eighty percent of those disenfranchised voters were black, Latino, or Asian. As a result, Brian Kemp stole our gubernatorial election in 2018 from us by a razor-thin margin over our beautifully enlightened sister from Spellman, Stacey Abrams.

Still, candidates like Stacey Abrams, Raphael Warnock, and Bakari Sellers give us hope that the political landscapes all over the South are ready for the earth to shift. If we could get just a few of our relatives we lost in the great migration, to northern cities, to move back to the South, it's possible I could finally win my next election! I ran for school board unsuccessfully and then city council unsuccessfully too.

Voting is an essential political power, but we can't stop there. We need people like you to run for political seats, ensuring that we have power that won't shrink in the face of the oppressive opposition you are certain to dine with, once you take your seat at the political table.

Be mindful that thou will prepare a table before you even in the presence of thine enemies. Win or lose, you will never fail as long as you keep trying. And who knows? I might, some sweet day soon, be able to convince my famous cousin from Chicago to move back to the dirty South, and then I know I will get to be our first black mayor in a peanut butter tan suit!

Anything is possible when we shift our mindsets. We the people can change our political landscapes as Mariah Parker, Park Cannon, and Nikema Williams have. Strong women in power are leading the way to our liberation, giving us the power to pass the John Lewis Voting Rights Act. Collectively, as we become more engaged, we will move our society on up.

OutKast said in the song "Elevators (Me and You)," "We are moving on up in the world like elevators." "Me and you," as Tony Toni Toné sang, means us collectively. *We are moving on up*'s origins came from this phrase sung in the theme song for the TV series *The Jeffersons*. George Jefferson, a black businessman from the south side of Chicago, became successful by owning a chain of dry-cleaning stores. In business, this was a lateral move that led George and his family to a vertical change in their residency. The theme song of *The Jeffersons* goes like this (and come on—feel free to sing it with me):

> Well, we're movin' on up to the east side.
> To a deluxe apartment in the sky.
> Movin' on up to the east side.
> We finally got a piece of the pie.
>
> Fish don't fry in the kitchen.
> Beans don't burn on the grill.
> Took a whole lotta tryin'
> Just to get up that hill.
>
> Now we're up in the big leagues,
> Gettin' our turn at bat.
> As long as we live, it's you and me baby.
> There ain't nothin' wrong with that.

Moving on up is economically aspirational, and in our communities, there ain't nothing wrong with that.

As you challenge yourself to rise in your situation, you may be asked to make some vertical moves. The calling for your own divine path may stretch you into doing something that no one else believes you can.

When life called for me to write this book as Barnard the Barber, people who had underestimated my abilities were skeptical. I kept getting asked the same questions: "You're writing a book? Well, who are you going to get to write it for you?" Yet and still, like Hamilton, I wrote my way out of all the negative energy.

In Paul Laurence Dunbar's poem he wrote *We Wear the Mask* of our tortured souls. Yet in the revelation of writing, your pen can turn you from a tortured soul into a transformational soldier!

So, as you read this, be mindful to get out of your own way; do something so big that the Almighty God will have to help you. Use this book as a reminder to you that He will. It costs nothing to tap into your passions. Inspired people are the ones who change the world. Be inspired, because inspiration is liberating and it is free!

We waste so much time and energy trying to impress people who may not even like us. We purchase things we really can't afford just to impress people we really don't know. Instead, spend your time filling your cup with things that fulfill you first, because it's truly a blessing to pour when your cup runneth over.

Then, once you meditate and tap into your passions, share your stories, because the universe will use your stories to inspire others. Elevating your community will be easier once you discover that the real prize gift in this world is you!

You've likely heard or read the Bible verse saying that it's easier for a camel to go through the eye of a needle, than it is for a rich man to get into the kingdom of heaven. But if a rich man can't make that flight, a poor man might not be able to afford a ticket to the United Kingdom either. Salvation is free, but can you afford a flight on Spirit while you are here?

I want you to receive the blessings in the prayer of Jabez, which says, "Oh bless me indeed, and enlarge my territory. That thy hand might be with me. And keep me from evil." God granted Jabez's request, and I know God will do the same for, "me and you, your mama, and your cousin too."

As we receive the blessings of the awakening, you must not be afraid to speak your mind. Our ancestors gifted us with their life's lessons. We don't need to reinvent the wheel here. The same God that worked for our ancestors will still work for us too! We only need to roll out our ancestor's measures to smooth out our transition, guiding our light into our brighter days. There is a plentiful harvest of progressive minds waiting on you to take the lead.

It is of upmost importance for you to build your dream team. You only need to surround yourself with just a few righteous-minded people to combat all of the negative noise. I'll bet that everyone under the sound of my weak voice has been at or has access to a hair salon somewhere in your community? The networks for our infrastructure have been established for centuries.

Back in the 1990s, at the Bronner Brothers Hair Show, I realized how connected we all are through the hair-care industry. Today we are more attached than ever. Utilizing social media, we are connected with stylists and activists in every corner of the globe. Understanding our power to unite lets you elevate your circumstances no matter where you are. There's power in knowing that we are not alone, and that the initial spark resides within you!

We want to see black-owned businesses do well, because they are our sources of inspiration. Our black-owned businesses hire people in our communities that other people won't. Elevating these centers in our communities through collective economics is the key to the realization of our revelation. See there now? You've got me rhyming like the Reverend Jesse Jackson.

The revelation of our coming to prominence as a people was written a long time ago. We will get our turn at last. Like this book was orchestrated and written before I ever sat down to write a word. *Maktub*.

Maktub is an Arabic word that means "It is written." We are the head, not the tail, and we have to see ourselves in that light. You can create your own positive postulates to get your life to where your heart truly desires for you to be.

Be always mindful of the power of your words. Because the talented poet Tupac Shakur wrote, "My every move is a calculated step, to bring me closer, to embrace an early death." We still don't know who killed our well-intending brother. But we do know by what we just read in his lyrics that this talented young brother, with his own words, just shot himself.

Today, we must get the language right. Be as the Godfather of Soul, James Brown, sang, "Yes, I'm black, and I'm proud!" I'm black and beautiful! Our steps are beautifully ordered by the divine. No matter where you are, know who you are. Know whose you are. And be proud to be unapologetically you.

Bu (Be you) is the most powerful element. *Bu* is not on the periodic table of elements, because it is the essence of your soul. Even when life has you caught at a crossroads while waiting on a stalled train, let your rejoicing rise as high as the listening sky. The grinding metal on the tracks may be loud, but keep lifting your voice, because the sky is listening.

The philosophy called Garveyism inspired the great Bob Marley to write, "Emancipate yourself from mental slavery. None but ourselves can free our minds." Therefore, no matter which corner of the globe you are from, the world's awakening is waiting for you!

As we part for now, I would be remiss if I didn't leave you with another important southern rule: if you see a man working in his yard, don't invade his sacred space unless it's a complete emergency. A man's most meditative times occur when he's riding his lawnmower. Most of the content in this book came to me in the middle of cutting grass.

Therefore, if you see a man at peace, working in his yard, could you please just let him be? It's hard enough for a black man to find a peaceful space anywhere else in this world. Those who don't understand this rule will just come up to you with a list of prying, frivolous and useless questions. Concluding the southern rule is this: never bother a man on a tractor because, some things are still sacred in the South!

Acknowledgments

I send a special thanks to Charlamagne Tha God for writing *Black Privilege: Opportunity Comes to Those Who Create It*. Your book showed me that readers do care about black men whose stories rode to town from the rural dirt roads of America too. That book was the format that guided my story. Although I must clarify for copyright infringement purposes, your book is in eight principles, while my story, *The Southern Awakening*, is in eight postulates.

They are not the same! Your book is by Charlamange Tha God and my book is by Barnard the Barber. Do you see the difference? It's like McDonald's and McDowell's. They are not the same! Although in all seriousness, our intentions are similar in hoping to inspire others to live in their truths! Thank you for providing a blueprint that made it possible for me to share my story.

I thank Stan Tucker, the founder of the nonprofit Leap for Literacy, a program designed to inspire children to tell their stories. It ended up causing this fifty-year-old kid to pen his first book. You are an amazing young man who has committed his life to inspiring others.

To the staff at the Boys and Girls Club in Winder, Georgia, you go way beyond what is required to make sure great futures start at the Boys and Girls Club.

To the youth at our Boys and Girls Club who learned to play chess under my tutelage and to those of you who ended up teaching me, never forget what we learned together, and keep believing our mantra: "I am smart! I am gifted! My next move will be my best move!"

I thank Brother Life and everyone with the nonprofit Chess and Community Conference for allowing me to branch out on your motto encouraging our youth to "Think before you move!"

To my geometry teacher, Ms. Cathy Borders, for believing that every child has genius in them. We just need to help our children find the genius that is within them. Though I may not be able to recite all the postulates and theorems you challenged me to memorize, but I do remember that if two parallel lines are cut by a transversal, alternate interior angles are congruent. In simple southern words, I am so thankful that God allowed our life's lines to intersect!

To my mentor in the NAACP, Johnny C. Smith, thank you for always trying to convince me that I am wrong, so I could learn to show when I am right.

To my English teachers at Athens Technical College: Ms. Ritter, Ms. Myers, and my night school professor, whose name I cannot remember, but you were so important to me that I am still searching to find your name. You all taught me the value of unstructured free writing. Because of that, people are reading this book. You all made me feel valued.

To my good counselor Mr. Leon Kincy, you were the first black man in my educational process to press me to turn a B into an A, and then an A into an A+, because a C was unacceptable. Even though we live in a world where some folks don't expect black people to do any better than that, you challenged me to understand that excellence is only a matter of doing my best.

East Athens Educational Dance Center, you are the gem in our community. Your staff inspires our kids to dream big, and you all have inspired me greatly. Mrs. Lois Thomas Ewing, what a founding gift EAEDC is and will always be. To Nina Billups and the late Ronnie Anderson, your selflessness will be felt by us forever.

Ballethnic Dance Company's Nena Gilreath and Waverly Lucas, your partnership with EAEDC in pursuit of excellence moves mountains to tears. We admire your dedication to hard work, to dance, and to the development of our youths' minds, bodies, and souls.

Archway Publishing's Josie McGraw, Tamar Lane, and Jeff Stevens paved the path for this first-time author born and raised in the sticks to become a *New York Times* best seller with Simon and Schuster, which brought this book up to its standards. You make masterpieces!

I thank my cousin Mont for seeing the greatness in me as a seed, and I thank Teddy Patty for watering those thoughts. No one gets anywhere without somebody. And my somebody is you.

I cannot ever give thanks enough to my cousin Spank for saving my life. You have the kind, giving spirit of your mom, my dear beautiful and sweet Cousin Pearly.

Thank you, Sharon McCoy. You are the first human being I chose to read my book, because your kind words validated the writer in me that I never believed existed, until my written words met you. As kindred spirits, we first connected through working with kids in chess. Outside of that, as a contributing editor at Humor in America, when you said, "I really enjoy reading your posts," your few words, plus our shared understanding of the importance of laughter, gave me all the encouragement I needed to write the *Southern Awakening*.

Thanks also to the following:

> Bronner Brothers
> Flanigan's Portrait Studio
> Volunteer Rebar
> Ellis Rogers Cement Construction Company
> Deborah Gonzales and Open Records
> Slow Rollers Motorcycle Club
> Russell Trucking Company
> Attorney Ken Dious
> Tonza Sheree Thomas and Hot 706.6
> Visions Hair Salon

Razor's Edge Barber Shop

Master's Touch

The Honorable Mr. Herman Sheats, his Lovely wife Candace, and their precious daughter Barbara (Babs). Sheats Barber and Beauty has always been the source of inspiration for our community.

The Golden Comb, Pam Haynes & Irish Gresham

Mark and Company

Marcus Blades

Styles by Stacee

Studio 74 Styling Shop, LLC CEO, Doonkie Dean of Winder Barber Academy

RSVP Studio and Hair Company

Eberhart and Son Mortuary

V-103.3

WXAG 92.7 FM and 1470 AM

Lady B, Barbara Sims, B.a. Sims (on Facebook)

Michael Thurmond

Walter Allen and Walter Allen Jr.

The *Zebra* Magazine

Ron Carson Jr. Editor & Chief of *Highlight* Magazine

Garrick Dixon

Kountry Wayne

Dr. Angela Moton

Statham Elementary Principal Dr. Salethia James

Art Chat Daddy Sims

City of Statham Police Department

City of Statham Police Chief Ira Underwood

Norman Garrett, City of Monroe

Marjorie Farms

Elders Cleaners

Chae's Candy Casino

Out Da Stixx Productions

Statham Public Library

Hillman-Rainwater Park
Mario Tory
Keso Crazae
Madam Stushstyles
Desi Banks
The Hair Doctor at Jason's II
Wilson's Styling Shop
Tamara Johnson Shealy
Diamond Ministries
The Ida B. Wells Museum
Tiana Ferrell
Roots of the Spirit
Little Rock Nine Museum
Sims Towing
360 Jeezy
Kenny Duncan
Dwayne Boyd Photography
The Glenwood Alumni Association
The National Association for the Advancement of
Colored People
The National Action Network
Joe Madison, The Black Eagle
Dudley's Hair Care Products
Shekinah Jo Anderson
Alexis Scott and *Atlanta Daily World*
Premier Actors Network and Dwayne Boyd
Donnie Creightney Concrete Company
Lil Ice Cream Dude
Dotson's Janitorial Services
Kathy's Kitchen
Long Janitorial Cleaning Service Inc., Joann's Things,
     Shen Long Logistics, & The Long Way Fitness
Anthony Thurmond's Concrete Company
CJK Rentals

Adams Vending
Marcus Coleman and (SOS) Save OurSelves
Pop Up Tees
Attorney Ben Crump
Tammy Gibson "Honoring The Legacy"
Miss Lacy Studios, LLC

The Resurrection Teaser

The Resurrection is the second book by Barnard Sims, whose pen name is Barnard the Barber, following *The Southern Awakening*. *The Resurrection* is a guide to unite the untapped but unlimited potential of people of color in the South using five steps: Visualization, Activation, Organization, Elevation, and the Revelation. The Revelation is only the first step of Visualization in the flesh. Propelling off of the success of his first book, Barnard the Barber utilizes his validated platform as an elevated thinker to empower rural pockets of oppression that still exist down south. Due to the networking among cosmetologists, barbers, and nail technicians in salons in nearly every community, the infrastructure has been set for decades, yet their empowerment has lain dormant for years.

Now that you have experienced *The Southern Awakening*, the harvest is plenty, and our season is long overdue. And as my white friends would say, "The South will rise again"—but this time, collectively, we will guide the South to rise in the righteous way! As T.D. Jakes said, "Get ready. Get ready. Get ready!" It's always the perfect time for *The Resurrection*.

CPSIA information can be obtained
at www.ICGtesting.com
Printed in the USA
LVHW041800110723
752130LV00002B/59